W9-BDJ-071

BLACK BELT
TAE KWON DO

The Ultimate Reference Guide to the
World's Most Popular Black Belt Martial Art

BLACK BELT
TAE KWON DO

Yeon Hwan Park

Jon Gerrard

세계에서 가장인기있는

유단자무술참고서

☑®
Facts On File, Inc.

BLACK BELT TAE KWON DO
The Ultimate Reference Guide to the World's Most Popular Black Belt Martial Art

Checkmark Books
An imprint of Facts On File, Inc.
11 Penn Plaza
New York, NY 10001

Library of Congress Cataloging-in-Publication Data

Park, Yeon Hwan.
    Black belt taekwondo : the ultimate reference guide to the advance techniques of the world's most
    popular martial art / by Y. H. Park & Jon Gerrard.
       p. cm.
    ISBN 0-8160-4240-3 (hc) — ISBN 0-8160-4241-1 (pb)
    1. Tae kwon do. I. Gerrard, Jon. II. Title.

GV1114.9 .P355 2000
796.815'3—dc21   99–057876

Checkmark Books are available at special discounts when purchased in bulk quantities for businesses, associations, institutions or sales promotions. Please call our Special Sales Department in New York at (212) 967-8800 or (800) 322-8755.

You can find Facts On File on the World Wide Web at http://www.factsonfile.com

Text design by Joan M. Toro

Printed in the United States of America

VB FOF 10 9 8 7 6 5 4 3 2 1
   PB 10 9 8 7 6 5 4 3 2 1

This book is printed on acid-free paper.

CONTENTS

PREFACE

In the years since we wrote our first book, *Tae Kwon Do: The Ultimate Reference Guide to the World's Most Popular Martial Art,* many people have expressed their pleasure with the book as a reference guide and teaching aid. The one thing that each of them has commented on, however, is the lack of information on black belt techniques. When we wrote that first book, it was our intention to encompass only the color belt/student level techniques to provide beginning Tae Kwon Do students with a means to allow them to study and practice more effectively on their own. To our delight, the book has achieved that and more. Across the United States, and in other countries as well, many Tae Kwon Do masters use the book as a primer for their students. At all Y. H. Park Taekwondo Centers, students are encouraged to obtain a copy of the book to help them when practicing on their own—and the results are impressive. Students find ready answers by referring to the book, allowing them to work through forms or techniques on their own. Time and again we have seen students accelerate mastering the various techniques by using that book.

Now we have written this companion book for black belt–level practitioners. As with the first book we have included clear photographic representations of each technique and form to allow practitioners to work more effectively on their own. We want to emphasize, however, that no book can take the place of actual instruction. These books are intended to serve as study aids and sources of information. Pictures cannot replace the knowing eye of an experienced instructor. Written explanations cannot convey the same understanding of timing and focus imparted by a qualified master. In other words, you cannot become an instant black belt by reading this, or any other, book. However, students of the art will find these books to be valuable references on every aspect of the art.

Black belts are the leaders of the Tae Kwon Do community. Lower level practitioners look to them for guidance. It is expected that once a student reaches the level of black belt he or she will assist with the training of the lower belts. Traditionally, the rank of black belt has been understood to mean "advanced student," or one who has mastered all of the basic techniques. In fact, first to third degree black belts are addressed by the title *chokyonim,* which means "instructor." Understanding this, we have also included in this book sections on how to effectively teach Tae Kwon Do. Although a person may be an impressive martial artist, it doesn't automatically mean that teaching will come naturally to him or her. We have drawn upon our years of teaching experience to put together what we feel is a solid core of instructional approaches. As with the art itself, however, teaching is not something learned without proper training. Some students feel that merely achieving the level of black belt qualifies them to be teachers. A few even attempt to open their own schools. This is a mistake. Although they have earned the title of *chokyonim,* it is only under the watchful tutelage of a seasoned master that a person can learn to be an effective teacher. Even those gifted with natural teaching ability can benefit from apprenticing themselves to an experienced master. After all, it is your students who will suffer if you are not properly prepared to teach them.

Finally, we want to repeat the invitation we extended in our first book. To truly understand and appreciate Tae Kwon Do, one must experience it. Come, study and experience with us.

Grandmaster Yeon Hwan Park
Jon Gerrard

Grandmaster Park (center) and Mr. Gerrard (second from right) with the Y. H. Park instructor staff

ACKNOWLEDGMENTS

We want to thank the following people for graciously donating their time and efforts to help us make this book possible:

> Master Ha Young Cho
> Master Young S. Kim
> Master Brian C. Jang
> Master Keun H. Lee
> Instructor Seung M. Kim
> Earl Anderson

We would also like to extend a special thanks to Peter Kohn, who took all of the photographs that appear in the book.

Finally, we want to acknowledge the special assistance of Team-USA for their invaluable contribution to the sections on managing and marketing a Tae Kwon Do school.

I am pleased to give my enthusiastic endorsement to this book. I was immensely pleased when I learned that Master Park and Mr. Gerrard were working on a sister book to their original work, *Tae Kwon Do.* Their first book has become the definitive reference guide for Taekwondo practitioners around the world. And with good reason, Master Park and Mr. Gerrard have succeeded in concisely organizing the elements of our art into a single, easy-to-understand volume. Now they have done the same for black belt students.

This book is a worthy companion to their earlier work. Not only does it clearly illustrate the advanced level techniques, it also goes beyond a mere explanation of the physical techniques to include essential information on effective teaching and training practices. This will benefit both instructors and student alike. For anyone interested in running a school, the information they have put together on managing and marketing is invaluable. Anyone who considers himself a serious student of our art should make these books an essential part of his library.

Un Yong KIM
President

United States Taekwondo Union

One Olympic Plaza, Suite 405
Colorado Springs, CO 80909
Tel: (719) 578-4632
FAX: (719) 578-4642

It is with great pleasure that I give my strong endorsement to this book on the art of Tae Kwon Do. Like everyone else in the Tae Kwon Do community, I am very familiar with the first book written by Master Park and Mr. Gerrard. Its clear explanations of the basic techniques of our art have made it the instructional manual and reference guide of choice for a great many practitioners. Now they are bringing us this excellent book on Black Belt level techniques. This sequel has been long awaited by students and instructors alike.

Continuing where the original book left off, *Black Belt Tae Kwon Do* gives a comprehensive treatment of the advanced techniques of the art. I can think of no better books to recommend to anyone who wants to have a complete reference source for Tae Kwon Do. I give this book my highest recommendation.

Sincerely,

Sang Chul Lee
President, US Taekwondo Union

INTRODUCTION

Tae Kwon Do, the Korean art of unarmed fighting, has a long and proud history. Its earliest roots have been traced back more than 2,000 years to 50 B.C. when artists of the time incorporated images of fighters using classic Tae Kwon Do techniques in their work. Known in its earliest form as Taek Kyon, this fighting art has developed over the centuries since its creation into the deadly self-defense system and immensely popular international sport that it is today. But what is Tae Kwon Do? How is it different from other martial art systems? And why has it become such a renowned popular sport?

Tae Kwon Do literally means the art (*do*) of kicking (*tae*) and punching (*kwon*). But this is only the barest, most superficial definition of an intricate and complex art. Certainly, Tae Kwon Do is a system of unarmed self-defense, in which the practitioner uses parts of his or her body as weapons. Advanced level practitioners have the ability to shatter bone with a single kick or hand strike. But self-defense is only one aspect of our art. During the Silla dynasty in Korea (A.D. 668–A.D. 935), a group of traveling warriors known as the Hwarang were responsible for the spread of the system throughout the country. These nomadic warriors were not mere soldiers however. These were well-educated nobles dedicated to the highest of moral ideals. While Taek Kyon was incorporated into their basic education, the core of their learning was centered on Confucian philosophy and Buddhist morality. In all things, their actions were guided by a set of principles known as the Five Codes of Human Conduct that stressed loyalty and justice as the central tenets of a moral life. While very effective as a system of self-defense, this early form of Tae Kwon Do served mainly as a sport and recreational activity designed to improve the character of its practitioners. Since that time, Tae Kwon Do has remained an art centered on personal growth and moral improvement.

Although Tae Kwon Do shares some superficial traits in common with other martial arts, it can be differentiated from these other systems by certain very specific characteristics. To begin with, Tae Kwon Do relies predominantly on kicking techniques. As much as 70 percent of the techniques in our art are kicks. The added reach and strength of the legs make them superior at delivering powerful blows. Tae Kwon Do takes advantage of this by centering the majority of its techniques on leg attacks. Secondly, the kicking techniques of Tae Kwon Do are performed in a uniquely quick, snapping manner. Beginning by bending the leg into a tightly coiled position, the kicks of Tae Kwon Do snap out and back with a quickness not found in other systems. In addition to this, Tae Kwon Do makes use of a very mobile, upright fighting stance that allows for quick action on the part of the fighter. Unlike other systems that make use of deeper, more formal stances, Tae Kwon Do practitioners stand virtually upright. Although the lower, rigid stances of other systems do provide their practitioners with a high degree of stability, the philosophy of Tae Kwon Do is that it is better to be able to move quickly on your feet rather than to be firmly rooted in one place.

Tae Kwon Do's immense popularity as a sport is due to the unique and dynamic nature of its sparring competitions. By using lightweight padding that protects the wearer from serious injury yet still allows for virtually unrestricted movement, Tae Kwon Do fighters are free to throw virtually any technique with full power. This not only enables the competitors to move freely and use their techniques safely, but it affords spectators the opportunity to witness dazzling displays of acrobatic skill. The numerous high, jumping and spinning kicking techniques of Tae Kwon Do would quickly lead to serious injury without the protective gear now in use. With it, however, practitioners can give and receive numerous blows throughout the course of a match and continue to compete. This aspect of the art ultimately earned it a spot on the roster of international sports, including the Olympic Games. Today, Tae Kwon Do is practiced in 167 countries by an estimated 40 million people and is recognized as the most popular martial art system in the world.

Over the years, a number of different governing bodies have arisen with the aim of unifying Tae Kwon Do practitioners. For many years different styles of the art were practiced, each of which called itself Tae Kwon Do. Each of these different schools, or *kwans,* were based on the teachings of different masters who emphasized slightly different aspects of the art. Although a few of these *kwans* remain independent to this day, the vast majority of Tae Kwon Do schools have allied themselves under the jurisdiction of the World Taekwondo Federation (WTF), which is the only organization recognized by the Korean government as the international regulating body for Tae Kwon Do. Within each country outside of Korea, various governing bodies have been established under the auspices of the WTF (see appendix D). In the United States of America, all official Tae Kwon Do activities are governed by the United States Taekwondo Union (USTU). All of the information and techniques in this book refer to Tae Kwon Do as it is taught by the WTF/USTU.

This book has been written to provide information on the advanced techniques of the modern art of Tae Kwon Do. As such, we have assumed that the reader has a certain basic understanding of the art, and we have not taken the space to explain many of the more elementary principles and concepts. Our companion book to this work, *Tae Kwon Do*, covers all of the basic information and techniques beginning students (below the level of black belt) need to know. We encourage you to refer to the companion book if you are not already familiar with Tae Kwon Do so that you can gain the full benefits of this book.

1 Philosophy of Tae Kwon Do

Two thousand years ago, Korea was divided into three kingdoms: Silla, founded in 57 B.C.; Koguryo, founded in 37 B.C.; and Baekche, founded in 18 B.C. Of the three kingdoms, Silla was the smallest and had the least developed civilization. Established near the coast of the Korean peninsula, the small kingdom was constantly under attack by Japanese pirates. In desperation, Silla eventually asked for help from King Gwanggaeto in the neighboring kingdom of Koguryo, the largest and most powerful of the three kingdoms. King Gwanggaeto, the 19th of the Koguryo monarchs, knew that if the pirates were allowed to establish a foothold in Silla, they would pose a threat to the entire Korean peninsula. In response, the king sent a force of 50,000 soldiers to help its smaller neighbor drive out the pirates. It was during this joint campaign that the Koguryo soldiers were first exposed to a system of unarmed fighting known in Silla as Taek Kyon, the early precursor of modern Tae Kwon Do. Passed in strict secrecy to a few select Koguryo warriors by early masters of the art, Taek Kyon was eventually brought back to the court of King Gwanggaeto. The king was so impressed with what he saw that he ordered training in Taek Kyon to be incorporated into the formal education of the young nobility.

The warrior nobility of Koguryo were a very special elite group of men known as the society of the Hwarang-do ("the way of flowering manhood"). Selected between the ages of 16 and 20 for inclusion in this prestigious group, the members of the Hwarang-do were chosen from among the sons of the royal family, who served as the leaders, and the rest of the noble families who formed the main body of the order. As the leader class within their society these young men were gifted with the finest education. The value of a well-rounded education was appreciated by generations of the Koguryo monarchy, who understood that the welfare of their society depended on the wisdom of its leaders. Aside from such practical disciplines as history, swordsmanship, riding, archery and military tactics, the Hwarang-do were also instructed in ethics, Buddhist morality and Confucian philosophy. In particular, they had adopted the teachings of the Buddhist scholar Wonkang as the guiding principles for their way of life. Their life philosophy was centered on a set of principles known as the Five Codes of Human Conduct:

> Be loyal to your country
> Be obedient to your parents
> Be trustworthy to your friends
> Never retreat in battle
> Never make an unjust kill

To break any of these codes was unthinkable, because it was these codes that defined the essence of who and what the Hwarang-do were. When Taek Kyon was incorporated into their curriculum, it too became subject to the moral and philosophical principles that guided their lives. As such, while Taek Kyon remained an effective fighting system, its main purpose was to help perfect the characters of its practitioners. From that time until today, although the physical techniques and even the name of the art have undergone change, its core purpose has remained the same.

Today, modern Tae Kwon Do has expanded on the original Five Codes of the Hwarang-do, modifying them into what is now known as the Eleven Commandments of Tae Kwon Do:

> Loyalty to your country
> Respect your parents
> Faithfulness to your spouse
> Respect your brothers and sisters
> Loyalty to your friends
> Respect your elders
> Respect your teachers
> Never take life unjustly

> Indomitable spirit
> Loyalty to your school
> Finish what you begin

Along with mastering the physical techniques of our art, all Tae Kwon Do practitioners are expected to abide by these axioms. It is not unheard of for masters to withhold promotion from or even to demote a student who breaks one of the commandments. Like the original Hwarang-do, it is these principles that serve to identify all Tae Kwon Do practitioners as members of a unified group.

THE FIVE AIMS OF TAE KWON DO

The Eleven Commandments of Tae Kwon Do provide students with clearly defined, specific behaviors that every practitioner is expected to follow. In the real world, however, we understand that every possible situation cannot be anticipated and planned for with a list of set rules. Therefore, along with the 11 commandments, Tae Kwon Do includes in its teachings a set of behavior goals known as the Five Aims of Tae Kwon Do:

> Respect (of oneself and others)
> Humility
> Perseverance
> Self-control
> Honesty

Unlike the 11 commandments, which are specific rules, the five aims are purposefully general because they are intended as idealized behavior traits. Practitioners who take these guidelines to heart and earnestly practice them in their lives cannot help but follow the eleven commandments as well because the commandments were devised as specific expressions of these general principles.

THE PHILOSOPHY OF THE BELT SYSTEM

The first practitioners of Tae Kwon Do did not use a series of colored belts to indicate their progress. They did not have formal uniforms like the *dobok* worn by today's practitioners either. The clothing they wore were simple, loose-fitting garments that absorbed sweat and allowed them to move and kick freely, something like the warm-up sweats people wear today. In fact, the clothing they practiced in were actually the undergarments they wore beneath the outer clothes they would normally wear in public. Likewise, the belts they wore were simply there to keep their clothing in place and had no other significance. Over time as they practiced, however, their belts became dirtier and darker. Eventually, a dark belt came to symbolize someone who had been practicing the art for a long time and was therefore a person of advanced skill.

Today, a black belt still indicates a Tae Kwon Do practitioner with a high degree of skill. Below the level of black belt, the various belt colors not only serve as an outward indicator of a student's level of proficiency, but also serve to reflect the philosophical growth the student is undergoing. Tae Kwon Do seeks to attune its practitioners with the natural flow of the universe. One of the most fundamental expressions of this flow is the life cycle. All living things are born, go through a stage of growth until they achieve maturity, pass on the seeds of life for the next generation and then move on to the next plane of existence. The practice of Tae Kwon Do also follows this type of cycle. Students begin with no knowledge of the art, learn and develop their skills until they have mastered the art, and then pass on what they know to students who come behind them. It is this cycle of growth, development and passing of knowledge that the color of the students' belts reflects.

Although individual schools may still employ variations of belt colors, the World Taekwondo Federation has standardized the progression of belts and now recognizes five colors below black belt: white, yellow, green, blue and red. Beginning students wear a white belt. The lack of color symbolizes purity and innocence as reflected by their lack of knowledge of Tae Kwon Do. The next belt is yellow, symbolizing the rising sun, which is the source of all life. At this level, students are beginning to learn some of the basics of the art. The next belt is green, the color of growing things well rooted and reaching upward toward the sky. At this level students are beginning to develop power. Next is blue, the color of the sky, open and boundless, toward which growing things are reaching. At this level, students begin to stabilize their power and develop a focus to their studies as they reach out to achieve their potential. The last color before black is red, the color of blood, the vital essence of life. Students at this level are deepening their power and control. Finally, there is black belt. Black represents all of the colors combined. At this highest stage the mastery of techniques is reflected by calm dignity and sincerity.

THE PHILOSOPHICAL GOAL OF TAE KWON DO

Up to this point we have discussed various philosophical aspects of our art as expressed by such things as the Eleven Commandments, the Five Aims and the Belt System. But what is the common element among these things? From our examination of the historical roots of the art we know that the aim of Tae Kwon Do is to improve the character of its

practitioners. But what measure are we using to judge how a student is improving?

If we were to express the philosophical goal of our art in a single statement, it would be that Tae Kwon Do training is meant to bring its practitioners into harmony with the universe. Rooted in Buddhist teachings, the core philosophy of Tae Kwon Do is based on a view of the universe as a dynamic environment in a perpetual state of change in which opposite forces are contantly adjusting themselves to maintain the harmonious balance of the cosmos. There are eight of these opposing forces that represent the cyclical flow of the universe. Collectively these are known as the eight *kwaes,* or signs of divination. Each sign is represented by a symbol consisting of three parallel lines drawn one on top of the other, with some symbols having one or more lines cut in two. Each of the lines represents the three aspects of reality: the surface level, the middle level and the deep level. The surface level is the appearance, that which is most readily seen. The middle level represents the functional aspect of the object or substance. The bottom level represents the spiritual aspect. A solid line stands for perfection of that aspect, while a broken line represents imperfections in that aspect. Thus, heaven (*keon*) is represented by three unbroken lines, while its opposite, earth (*kon*) is represented by three broken lines.

By examining the above illustration, you will find each of these symbols placed around the circular *um* and *yang* sign. (Note that each symbol is oriented so that its top is away from the center of the *um* and *yang*, while the bottom is nearest to the circle.) *Um* and *yang* represent the fundamental opposing forces of the universe. There is no single way to interpret or define the concepts of *um* and *yang*. They stand for polar opposites and the specifics of their meaning can vary depending on the context. Traditionally, they have been applied to such paired opposites as light and dark, hard and soft, good and evil, and male and female. The symbol for heaven is positioned at the top of the diagram, with the other signs being read in order as you follow them counter-clockwise around the circle. Notice that each symbol is the exact opposite of the one directly across from it, with their meanings being opposite as well. Thus, heaven (*keon*) at the top is opposed by earth (*kon*) at the bottom, while fire (*ri*) on the left is opposed by water (*kam*) on the right. Taken as a whole this symbol is known as Tae Geuk, or Boundless Eternity, which symbolizes the universe.

The ultimate aim of Tae Kwon Do is to bring its practitioners into harmony with the universe. This harmony can only be achieved when opposite forces are distributed equally, resulting in balance. However, if one force dominates, the result is discord. Therefore, for Tae Kwon Do practitioners to live this harmony they must tailor their actions to their environment. For example, if an adversary directs aggressive energy toward one, the practitioner should respond by using passive or yielding energy and allow the adversary's energy to flow harmlessly past. The blocking motions of Tae Kwon Do are designed to follow this very principle. Instead of meeting an attack head on, the blocking techniques redirect an opponent's power to allow it to flow past.

To function on this level, however, it is necessary to rid oneself of the ego, or what is known as the "discriminating mind" in Zen Buddhism. It is the discriminating mind that constantly seeks to judge and evaluate, a process that removes the person from living in "present time." In that state a person operates without conscious thought, responding immediately and correctly to whatever situation he or she is presented with. Most people have had brief experiences when they operated in present time. Twisting the steering wheel of a car to avoid an accident at the last second, reaching out to grab or block something tossed in one's direction, or some other event in which a person reacts without thinking are all examples of this principle. Tae Kwon Do practitioners train themselves to be able to slip into this state of mind at will. People who live in present time are at peace with themselves and the world around them, regardless of the setting. Such people cannot be upset by anything they encounter in life. It is the ultimate aim of Tae Kwon Do for students to reach a point where they live their lives in a state of present mind.

2 Practicing Tae Kwon Do

Anyone who begins training in Tae Kwon Do does so with the same objective in mind—one day achieving the rank of black belt. Although the black belt does signify a person of advanced skill, the attainment of a black belt is not the end of training but rather the beginning of serious study. In the color belt ranks, students are learning the basic techniques of Tae Kwon Do. Even so, it can take several years of dedicated work before a person reaches first degree black belt. To achieve this level, students will develop mental and physical abilities that will enable them to break pine boards with a single blow or leap high in the air to kick a target many feet above the floor and land again under control. These are impressive feats to be sure, but for those students who continue their study of the art, even greater abilities are yet to be discovered.

In Tae Kwon Do, there are ten levels of black belt. Each level, known as a *dan,* represents not only the attainment of new skills, but the continuing perfection of the basic skills one has already learned. The study of Tae Kwon Do is a lifelong effort, based on the understanding that knowledge of the art is never truly complete. No matter how well one can do a technique, there is always a higher level of perfection that can

7

be achieved. Each kick can be more powerful, each punch more precise. Through continual practice, students of the art strive to refine what they know, seeking to bring themselves ever closer to the unattainable but always sought after ideal of ultimate perfection. Based on this philosophy, even grand masters can be said to be students of Tae Kwon Do.

When students reach the level of first degree black belt, or first *dan,* they are given the title of *chokyonim,* which means instructor. At this stage, a person is considered to have reached the minimum level of competence necessary to teach what he or she knows. In fact, it is expected that black belts will assist the master instructor with running classes. More than merely serving as an extra pair of eyes and hands to help with classes, however, the main reason that black belts teach is to further consolidate what they have already learned. There is no better way to develop a deep understanding of anything than to teach it. By having to demonstrate and explain the same techniques over and over again, black belts ultimately achieve a more profound knowledge of their art than they could ever do otherwise. This is because in order to teach something an instructor must constantly be coming up with new ways to get ideas across to different students, each of whom learns in a different way. This requires constant thinking about not only how the various techniques are done, but *why* they work. Once this is understood, that knowledge is then truly owned by the instructor.

In addition to seeking this deeper understanding of their art, new black belts are also working to improve their physical abilities as well. Through continual practice and drilling, reflexes are honed, speed is increased, strength and flexibility are improved. Although there are new techniques to be learned at each black belt level, greater mastery of the basic techniques is just as important. Physical training for black belts is aimed at developing refined control over the body. Black belts focus on combination techniques and multiple kicks in particular. The idea is for the body to become totally compliant to the will. Black belts strive to deliver attacking and defending techniques in any direction and combination. Tae Kwon Do practitioners are renowned for their ability to launch a flurry of kicks to targets at all different heights. If during a sparring or self-defense situation an opening to land a blow appears at a low target that is immediately followed by an opportunity to score against a high-level target, a Tae Kwon Do practitioner should be able to launch successful attacks to both targets using the same foot without returning the foot to the floor between techniques.

The other thing that black belts train for is to refine their focus—the ability to concentrate all of the power in their body to a single point in space. It is through the use of focus that Tae Kwon Do practitioners are able to perform breaking techniques. Whereas below the level of black belt, students develop the ability to break a few boards at a time, through ever-increasing control of focus black belts are able to smash through large piles of boards and even such things as concrete and brick. This enables one not only to throw multiple kicks with the same foot, but to do so with devastating results.

To develop this level of skill takes time. But for students who truly understand the commitment of their training, that time seems to pass quickly. Such people are not concerned with how long it takes for them to get there. They understand it is the process itself that is important. For students who continue to apply themselves to the study of their art, it will take a minimum of six years to rise from first *dan* to fourth *dan,* when they will earn the respected title of *sabomnim,* or master. By this time, knowledge of the techniques is deeply ingrained and instinctive. Fourth-degree black belts no longer require the supervision of higher ranking *dans* in order to teach. Their understanding of the basics of Tae Kwon Do is now considered complete. It is at the level of fourth *dan* that a black belt may open his or her own school. Yet one's own training continues.

Having achieved a deep and abiding understanding of the basic techniques of Tae Kwon Do, black belts from fourth *dan* and up are working toward the perfection of their technique and power. Pinpoint control of each technique is strived for and focus is refined even further. A master of Tae Kwon Do is capable of feats of agility and power that few others in the world can match. More than this, after years of observing students, dedicated training and self-study, a Tae Kwon Do *sabomnim* has achieved a level of perception that allows one to move with incredible ease against an opponent. From the barest hint of a movement, a *sabomnim* will know what an opponent is going to do and can react accordingly. It is this highly refined ability to "read" others that gives a *sabomnim* the seemingly clairvoyant ability to react almost before his or her opponent does.

It is said that you can tell the skill level of a Tae Kwon Do practitioner by the way the individual reacts in a fighting situation:

> A beginning student will block an attack.
> An advanced student will counterattack after blocking.
> A *sabomnim* does not need to block.

Promotion above the rank of sixth *dan* is a very special event. Black belts who hold a rank of seventh *dan* or higher are known as *kwanjangnim,* or grand master. To test for any rank above sixth degree, the practitioner must travel to the Kukkiwon itself, the headquarters of the World Taekwondo Federation in Seoul, Korea. There, the candidate will be judged by a panel of grand masters who comprise the

Kukkiwon Promotion Test Commission. In order to earn promotion at this level, the candidate must not only demonstrate technical skill, but also show some significant contribution to the art itself.

Finally, the highest level it is possible to achieve, that of tenth *dan,* is an honor bestowed upon a select few. Unlike other promotions, there is no mandatory waiting period or demonstration of skills required. Such an award is made by a decision of the Promotion Test Commission and is reserved only for those most dedicated practitioners who have devoted their lives to the furtherance of their art.

THE TRAINING HALL

The training hall, or *dojang,* is where the learning of Tae Kwon Do takes place. In the *dojang* students work as members of a community to constantly improve themselves. As such it is deserving of serious re-

spect by the students and any guests to the school. Demonstrating this respect is the reason that we bow whenever entering or leaving the training area. Some people have misconceptions about this, however. They often mistake respect for the place where we train with some form of religious reverence. While many students do ultimately come to experience a sense of spiritual growth through their study, Tae Kwon Do is *not* a form of religious worship. Through rigorous training students of Tae Kwon Do strive to improve themselves physically, mentally and spiritually.

For Tae Kwon Do training to be effective, however, there are certain things that a *dojang* needs to have. Most important is adequate space. Although any open space can serve as a training area, there are some basic amenities that will enhance practice sessions. To begin with, the space must be large enough to allow the students to move freely without being squeezed in on top of one another. For an average class of fifty students we recommend a rectangular area no less than 25 feet wide and 70 feet long (1,750 square feet). The rectangular shape of the *dojang* is not only traditional but practical as well. When students are lined up formally, they are arranged side by side in rows facing one of the long walls. The highest ranking students are in the front rows arranged in descending order of seniority from left to right (right to left from the students' perspective). This gives each student enough personal space to punch and kick without worrying about hitting another student and allows the instructor to see each student easily. This arrangement also allows the less advanced students to watch the higher belts when they are doing basic drills. If it is later necessary to divide the class for certain activities, the *dojang*'s length can be cut in half to allow for different types of training to take place at each end of the room without disturbing the other half of the class

Next is the proper floor. It should of course be level and flat, without any unexpected bulges or depressions that can result in stubbed toes or twisted ankles. Since numerous Tae Kwon Do techniques involve spinning and jumping, most schools cover their floors with some type of padding to help protect students if they fall. If the floor is covered, the padding must not have a spongy feel or be covered with soft plastic (such as a wrestling mat). This kind of padding can cause feet to get stuck in place. If students try a spinning technique on such a surface, they can easily catch toes and dislocate them, twist an ankle or even injure a knee.

Mirrors are a necessity. Students can learn a great deal by watching themselves in a mirror as they perform a technique. Having an instructor comment on technique is essential for any student's progress. But when students can watch themselves in a mirror and check what they are doing, understanding of the use of the body will be greatly enhanced. People often have difficulty telling how they are actually performing a technique by "feel" alone. When they see what the body is doing, however, and connect that to the way it feels, the sense of one's own body mechanics increases dramatically. To get the greatest benefit possible from the mirrors, they should be as large as possible. Many schools have entire walls covered with mirrors. Aside from enabling students to watch their own progress, mirrors also help make the practice area appear larger and brighter. One thing you should avoid is placing mirrors directly opposite each other. If the practice hall is especially narrow and the mirrors are close together, it can cause an infinite reflection effect that can be distracting and unsettling to some people.

Another thing that is very important is sufficient lighting. The entire *dojang* should be clearly and evenly lit. This is especially important during sparring sessions in which a student must react in a split second to what an opponent is doing. If one can't see what is coming, the individual can't react properly and someone could be hurt. Lights should be spaced so that they evenly illuminate the practice area without being blindingly bright. Fluorescent lights provide a soft, even light without generating excess heat. In addition to sufficient overhead lighting, many schools also have large windows on one side. This lends the space a wide open feel as opposed to the claustrophobic atmosphere of a completely enclosed space. Even if the practice area is large, lack of windows can give the school a closed-in, cavelike feeling.

Numerous pieces of training equipment are available to help martial artists develop and enhance their skills. Some equipment is very flashy and impressive-looking, but often without any serious value.

The best way to judge a piece of equipment is to ask yourself how it can be used to help develop skills. Since Tae Kwon Do is primarily concerned with striking techniques, all that is truly needed are different types of striking targets. In general, two types of training aids are useful to Tae Kwon Do students. The first is fixed striking pads. These usually take the form of small pads that can be mounted on a pole or wall, which students use to practice their punching and kicking. Since the pads are attached to an immovable surface, they are useful to help students develop not only power but a sense of spatial relations as well. Because these pads are small, usually no larger than a foot high and four to six inches wide, students must aim their blows carefully. Landing a jumping, spinning back kick squarely on such a pad requires a high degree of precision. Another type of fixed pad is a heavy bag. Usually hung from a chain, heavy bags offer students a person-sized target they can strike from 360°. Because it is so big, students do not have to be as precise with their techniques as they do with the smaller, mounted pads. However, the slight mobility it has because it is suspended gives students the chance to judge how powerful their techniques really are. A quickly snapped kick may look impressive, but only a truly powerful technique will make the heavy bag move.

Portable striking pads are the other type of training aid needed. Unlike fixed pads, portable pads are held by a partner to provide a moving target. Some of the most common are focus mitts and kicking pads. Focus mitts are thick pads worn glovelike on the hands by a partner while the student practices punching and/or kicking at them. These are extremely versatile pads that can be moved rapidly from one place to another. A quick twist of the partner's wrist will also change the angle of the striking surface, thereby forcing the student to change the angle of attack. Because they are worn on the hands, focus mitts do offer a degree of resistance to a strike. The one drawback to these pads are that powerful kicking techniques can severely shock the holder's arm, especially the elbow. Kicking pads are also handheld, but are more flexible than focus mitts. Consisting of little more than a double-sided pad with a projecting handle, they allow students to throw full power kicks with no shock to the holder's arm. Although they offer little resistance to a kick, they serve nicely as targets that can be individually adjusted to the reach of each student.

PRACTICE ROUTINES

Properly structured Tae Kwon Do classes all have the same basic structure. Once the students have been lined up according to rank, bows are exchanged between the students and the instructor(s). This establishes the tone of the class and serves as an indicator that the instruction is beginning. Next should follow a short period of meditation. When done properly, meditation clears the mind of distractions and relaxes students so that they can focus all their attention on the class. After meditation, the first activity should always be some form of warm-up and stretching exercises to prepare the body and help prevent injury, with special emphasis on stretching the legs and groin. Next, the class should practice basic blocking, punching and kicking as a group. No matter how high in rank a student rises, practicing basics is essential. Although advanced-level techniques seem far more

sophisticated than the basic ones, these basics form the foundation of all the other techniques. Incorporated into even the most advanced techniques are movements taken from the most fundamental ones. Through repeated practice of these basic motions, students develop the instinctive reflexes enabling them to use all of their techniques effectively.

After basics, the main body of the class begins. At this point the instructor devotes the remainder of the practice time to either one-steps (see below), self-defense techniques, forms or sparring. Many schools hold several different specialty classes each day to allow students to choose the type of workout they are most interested in. While it is possible to focus on more than one specialty in a class, to do more than two in the same session may not allow enough time to adequately train and can overtire the students. When the class is finished, students should once again line up according to rank and exchange bows with the instructor(s).

One-Steps

One-steps are formal drills in which a pair of students train together to develop effective fighting combinations. One student takes the role of the attacker and initiates a confrontation, while the other student takes the role of the defender and counters the attack with a prearranged response. While self-defense tactics in real-life situations should be spontaneous reactions to the specifics of the actual attack, one-steps represent proven, practical ways to deal with many common attacks. Because both students know what the attack and counter will be, their focus is not on speed or power but rather on making the series of

movements smooth and automatic. Then, should the student ever be faced with an attack like the one practiced, the reaction will be automatic and effective.

Each drill begins in the same way. The students start by facing one another and bowing. Next, they each adopt a ready stance. The person in the role of the attacker will then step *back* into a front stance and give a *ki-hop* to let the partner know it is time to begin. The defender gives a *ki-hop,* telling the attacker that he or she is ready. The attacker can then either throw the attacking technique immediately, or may wait several seconds before beginning to move. Although the exact attack and counter are known ahead of time, by having the attacker wait adds an element of uncertainty to the drill. When the attacker does eventually move, the defender's response will be a bit more realistic.

Due to their practical value, many Tae Kwon Do schools incorporate a set series of one-steps in their curriculum and require students to learn several of them for each promotion test. When doing one-steps, the attacks and responses should vary, with the techniques geared to the appropriate skill level of the students. We have included a sample of twelve advanced-level one-steps to illustrate a diverse range of effective counters. For the purposes of illustrating these techniques, the attacker will always appear on the left and attack with a right hand punch to either the high section (head) or middle section (body).

Technique #1: high section punch

a) right inner arm block,

b) & c)   left spinning elbow strike to the solar plexus,

d) left back-fist strike to the face,

e) right reverse punch to the face.

Technique #2: middle section punch

a) simultaneous left palm block and wrist capture with right knife-hand strike to the neck,

b) right knife-hand strike to the forearm,

c) right knife-hand strike to the side of the jaw.

Technique #3: middle section punch

a) left inner arm block,

b) right elbow strike to the ribs,

c) left elbow strike to the side of
    the jaw,

d) grab opponent by the shoulders,

e) knee strike to the middle
    section.

Technique #4: middle section punch

a) right inner arm block,

b) right back fist to the face,

Technique #4 (con't.)

c) left knuckle strike to the septum,

d) right ridge-hand to the temple.

Technique #5: high section punch

a) simultaneous right rising knife-hand block with left reverse punch to the ribs,

b) capture and twist attacker's arm with the right hand,

c) right side kick to the side of the knee.

Technique #6: high section punch

a) high X-block,

b) capture attacker's wrist and twist arm straight,

c) grab back of collar with the right hand and raise the captured arm,

Technique #6 (con't.)

d) force captured arm up and across attacker's back to throw,

e) left axe kick to the head.

Technique #7: high section punch

a) left knife-hand block,

b) simultaneous capture attacker's wrist with right reverse punch to the face,

c) right front kick to the middle section.

Technique #8: high section punch

a) left knife-hand block (note: defender sidesteps to the right),

b) simultaneous left wrist capture with right arc-hand attack to the throat,

Technique #8 (con't.)

c) right leg sweep,

d) right punch to the side of
    the jaw.

Technique #9: high section punch

a) simultaneous left knife-hand
    block with right knife-hand
    strike to the side of the neck,

b) simultaneous left wrist
    capture with left step,

c) & d)   right knife-hand strike to the back of the knee,

e) right punch to the side of
    the jaw.

Technique #10: high section punch

a) simultaneous left wrist capture with right wrist strike to the chin,

b) simultaneous twist and pull captured arm with left side step,

c) right side kick to the side of the knee.

Technique #11: middle section punch

a) left outside crossing kick block,

b) right front kick to the middle section,

c) right roundhouse kick to the head.

Technique #12: middle section punch

a) right inside crossing kick block,

b) & c) left spinning back kick to the middle section.

3 Advanced Techniques

Strictly speaking, there are no new techniques to be learned once a practitioner has reached the level of black belt. This does not mean, however, that there is nothing more to learn. Advanced practicing in Tae Kwon Do mainly consists of perfecting the basic techniques and learning to *apply* them in new ways. This can take years of dedicated work. To begin with, it is impossible to perfect a technique in the absolute sense. Although training will improve the way a practitioner performs any given technique, further fine-tuning of each technique can always be done. Advanced Tae Kwon Do training involves a series of steps in which the practitioner sets higher and higher goals. Once a higher level of performance is reached, a new goal is set, and so on.

From a practical standpoint, however, there are certain special skills that black belts train their bodies to do. Specifically, there are three core skills that black belts work at developing: multiple kicks, focus and simultaneous techniques. Multiple kicks are performed with the same foot without returning it to the floor. This is actually a lot more difficult than it seems. By the time a student reaches first *dan,* he or she has developed the ability to throw powerful kicks to head height and higher. But throwing a single kick to the head when you can wind up and bring your foot all the way up from the floor is much easier than throwing a second kick when your leg is already halfway to the target. Like all human movement*, whenever one foot is off the floor, the person is off balance, even if only for an instant. Black belts train to master their balance so that they can kick and retract their legs over and over. This takes a combination of coordination, strength and limberness.

With the kicking leg held up in a tightly coiled, bent position, there is also no chance to build momentum, which is one of the main forces used to generate power in a strike. Without momentum, the only way to get power into a technique is by using focus. This is the second core ability that black belt level practitioners work to perfect. Focus is the ability to channel all of the power in your body to a specific point in space. It involves more than just pure physical strength. Focus is developed through a combination of precisely controlled movement and relaxation. Although it seems contradictory, by completely relaxing the muscles before striking it is possible to initiate movements with incredible speed, thereby increasing power. The only time tension should enter the body is at the moment of impact. To then maximize the power generated, it is necessary to move the limbs in very precise ways. Like channeling water through a hose, the most powerful stream is created when the hose is straight and unkinked and when the spout is contracted to a small opening. Although there can be immense pressure behind the water, that force can be greatly reduced or even cut off altogether if the hose is bent and kinked. Likewise, if the spout is opened too wide, the stream is scattered and undirected. Applying this analogy to the human body, power can be generated through exercise (to build strength) and relaxation (to maximize speed). This is the pressure in the hose. To release that power, the limbs must move in the right way so that there are no "kinks" to inhibit the flow of energy. This is the reason Tae Kwon Do practitioners hold fists palm up at the belt and twist them palm down when punching. The twisting motion allows the arm to move most freely through the full range of the punch. Finally, the momentary tensing of the muscles at the moment of impact helps to concentrate the force of the blow, like closing a spout to a small hole.

Simultaneous techniques comprise the other skill black belts work to develop. Blocking attacks to both the high and low sections of the body at the same time or counterattacking at the same moment that an opponent's attack is blocked are examples of this. While high-ranking color belts are exposed to this concept in Tae Geuk Chil-Jong and Tae Geuk Pul-Jong, it is not until the level of black belt that Tae Kwon Do

---

* See the chapter **Sparring Techniques** for more information on the nature of human movement.

practitioners begin to truly refine simultaneous techniques. The primary way that black belts develop these techniques is through the practice of forms. Black belt–level forms contain numerous simultaneous techniques, whether they are simultaneous blocks, simultaneous blocks and counterattacks, or simultaneous attacks. In this way, Tae Kwon Do practitioners armor themselves against attacks from multiple opponents.

MEDITATION

To perform any physical activity in the best way possible, it is important for the mind to be completely focused on what you are doing. If your thoughts are on something else or if you allow yourself to be distracted, you will not give your best performance no matter what the activity. Tae Kwon Do requires a high degree of concentration. Even for masters, for whom the techniques of Tae Kwon Do are virtually instinctive, concentration is extremely important. One way to help focus the mind is through the use of meditation.

During meditation the practitioner seeks to bring about a state of "oneness," or *ill yo,* where thought and action are one and the same. Also known as "present time," this state of consciousness occurs when a person is able to completely tune out all surrounding activity and concentrate exclusively on what one is doing. Buddhist masters practice meditation for years in an attempt to develop this state of awareness. While the achievement of this ultimate level of control can take a lifetime of devoted practice, great benefits can be achieved through more modest practice.

Begin by sitting in a comfortable position with the back straight. With your eyes closed you should first concentrate on relaxing your body. This is a *passive* process. You cannot force yourself to relax, rather you must allow your body to relax. Once the tension has been allowed to drain away, you can then concentrate on emptying your mind of all thoughts. Again, this is a passive process that will not work if you attempt to force it to happen. One way to relax both mind and body is to pay attention to your breathing. Simply notice it. Do not try to control it. As you pay attention to your breathing you will find that you will relax and your breathing will become slower and shallower. After several minutes of meditation you will find that you feel refreshed and alert. You will then be better prepared to concentrate on your practicing.

FALLING

Although formal Tae Kwon Do does not permit sweeping* or throwing techniques during sparring, there may be occasions when students find themselves falling nonetheless. If a student is kicked powerfully enough or loses balance while attempting a jumping or spinning technique, he or she can end up hurtling toward the floor. There are also numerous self-defense techniques in which an opponent is tripped or thrown down. To help prevent injury during practice it is important that students learn to fall correctly.

Front Fall

When falling face first toward the floor, both hands should be brought up before the body (a) and slapped down against the floor so that the entire lower arm from elbow to palm strikes the floor at the same time (b). The slapping is important to absorb the force of the impact. It is extremely important that you do not hit with the elbows themselves,

a   b

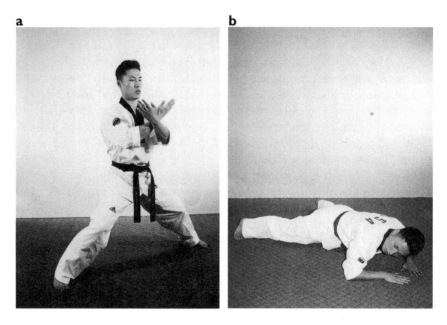

* Sweeping techniques involve the sudden pulling of a foot from under an opponent.

or severe injury to the joints can result. You also do not want to try to catch yourself "push-up style." If you are falling with a great deal of force, you will put strain on your elbow and shoulder joints if you simply try to catch yourself in this way. By keeping the elbows out and spreading the feet apart, a stable base is formed. Notice how the head is turned to one side and positioned directly above the hands. This protects the face from injury if the shock of the fall causes the head to impact the floor.

Back Fall

When falling toward your back, the arms are raised in front of the body in the same manner as in a front fall (a). Just as your body is about to strike the floor, slap out with both arms at the same time so that the entire arm from shoulder to palm strikes the floor at once (b). To be effective the arms must neither be straight out from the body or held

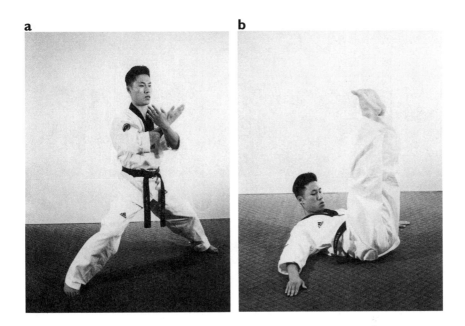

tightly against it. They should strike at 45° angles out from the torso. It is extremely important that the arms be kept rigidly straight as you slap. If the arms are bent, you will strike the floor with your elbows and cause severe damage to the bones. Notice also that the chin is kept tightly tucked into the chest to prevent the back of the head from striking the floor.

Side Fall

When falling to the side, the arm on the side of the body that you are falling to is extended while the opposite arm is pulled in to your side (a). As you fall, pull the extended arm across your body (b) and slap out so that the entire arm from shoulder to palm strikes the floor at once (c). To be effective the arm should strike at a 45° angle from the body. Again it is extremely important that the arm be kept rigidly straight as you slap to prevent injury to the elbow. Notice how the chin is tucked tightly into the chest here as well to prevent the head from being whisplashed against the floor.

a   b   c

Rolling Side Fall

In an instance in which you are falling forward and have enough control to tuck your body into a forward roll, you can use this fall. Extend one arm so that hand touches the floor first (a). This hand will help guide the rest of the fall. Be sure you turn your fingers in toward the center of your body and bend your elbow slightly to roll down along your arm. As you roll forward (b), tuck your chin in to the opposite shoulder and twist your body so that the line of your roll carries you from your shoulder across to the opposite hip (c). As you roll to that hip, slap out with the other arm just as you would in a normal side fall (d).

a　　　　　　　　　　**b**

c　　　　　　　　　　**d**

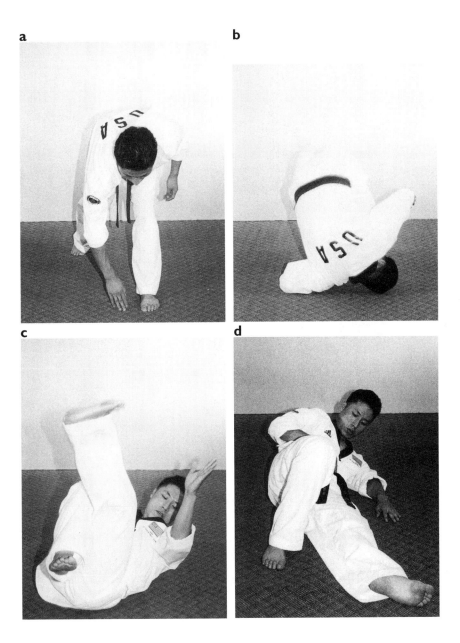

Diving Side Fall

This fall is used in extreme cases in which you are being hurtled forward with great force or are forced to hurtle an obstacle. As you leave the ground (b), reach out with your hands to help direct your fall. Whichever hand touches the ground first is your lead hand (c). Tuck your chin into the opposite shoulder and roll through the rest of the fall (d), (e) as you would do in a normal rolling side fall.

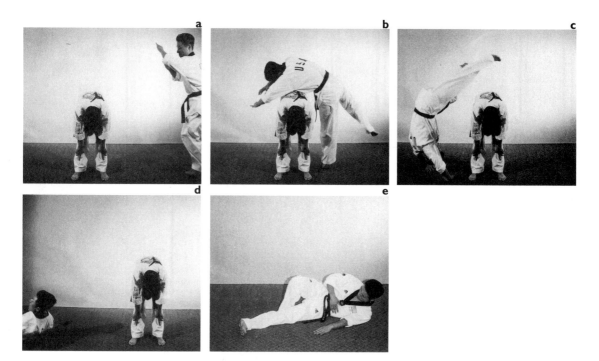

TECHNIQUES

As we stated earlier, the advanced techniques of Tae Kwon Do are essentially new applications of the basic techniques. Mainly, these consist of simultaneous techniques in which two things are done together: double defenses, double attacks, simultaneous defending and attacking. Those techniques we have included here are the ones formally taught to practitioners. Please note that while we have shown the techniques being performed in specific stances, most of them can be done from any stance.

Containing Vital Energy Stance

In this technique, the practitioner concentrates on focusing one's life force energy into the right fist, which is covered and contained by the left hand. This technique is used to hold built-up power in check to be released later. This technique is only performed using this stance.

Kumkang Block

This technique takes its name from the famous statue discovered in the Muyong-chong royal tomb, which dates back to 50 B.C. The simultaneous rising block and down block protect against attacks to the upper and lower areas while the raised foot is coiled in preparation for a counterattack. This technique is only performed using this stance.

Mountain Block

This technique uses an outer arm block in combination with an inner arm block to protect against simultaneous attacks to the upper area from opposite sides. The technique is performed by raising the arms into the position shown and then stepping to rotate the shoulders 180° while maintaining the arms in this position.

Partial Mountain Block

This technique uses an outer arm block in combination with a down block to protect against simultaneous attacks to the upper and lower areas from opposite sides. Although we have shown this technique using open hands, it can also be performed with fists.

Supported Inner Arm Block

In this technique, an inner arm block is assisted by bringing the opposite hand across the front of the body to protect against attacks to the middle section.

Supported Outer Arm Block

In this technique, an outer arm block is assisted by bringing the opposite hand across the front of the body to protect against attacks to the middle section. Note that in photograph (b) the fist is turned palm down. This allows for quick grabbing of an opponent's wrist following a block.

Scissors Block

This technique uses an outer arm block in combination with a down block to protect against simultaneous attacks to the upper and lower sections from the front.

Arc-Hand Strike

This technique uses the crescent-shaped area formed between the index finger and thumb as a striking surface. The two targets for this technique are the throat or the chin. If the throat is attacked, it is likely that the windpipe will be crushed. Attacking the chin will cause the jaw to be dislocated.

Hook Punch

This technique is used to deliver a punch at a right angle to the front of the body. From chamber position at the belt, the punching hand is fired out like a normal punch, but quickly hooks across the front of the body until it stops as shown. This technique requires a good control of focus to be effective.

Rising Block Punch

This technique uses a rising block in combination with a forward punch to block an attack to the upper section while simultaneously counterattacking. Note that although we have shown the technique using a jab punch, the technique can also be performed using a reverse punch.

Rising Block Palm-Heel Strike

This technique uses a rising block in combination with a palm strike to block an attack to the upper section while simultaneously counterattacking. Note that although we have shown this technique using a knife-hand for the rising block, it can also be performed using a fist. The difference is that when doing a knife-hand rising block the edge of the hand is the blocking surface. This requires precision in blocking, but gives you the opportunity to grab the opponent's wrist.

Rising Block Knife-Hand Strike

This technique uses a rising block in combination with a knife-hand strike to the side of the neck to block an attack to the upper section while simultaneously counterattacking. As in the previous technique, either the knife-hand or a fist can be used for the rising block. Due to the nature of human anatomy, the counterattacking knife-hand is only effective when done to the side of the neck as illustrated. Any other (knife-hand) attacking movement done in combination with the rising block will be awkward and ineffective.

Grabbing Uppercut

This technique uses an uppercut punch in combination with grabbing the opponent's clothes to pull the opponent close to deliver an attack. Usually done immediately following a blocking technique (the most common being an outer arm block), the blocking hand grabs the attacker's clothes to pull the person close while the rear hand delivers a punishing uppercut.

Two-Hand Punch

This technique uses both hands to deliver simultaneous punches. Two-hand punches can be delivered as normal forward punches (a) or as uppercuts (b).

Double Knife-Hand Strike

This technique uses both knife-hands to deliver simultaneous strikes to opposite sides of the target. The most common targets for this technique are the sides of the head and the body.

VITAL POINTS

Strikes and kicks are most effective when delivered to the weakest points of an opponent's body. Below we have pinpointed specific areas of the human body that are most vulnerable to attack.

Front of Body

1. Bridge of nose: A strike to this area can result in broken bones and disorientation.
2. Temple: A strike to this area can result in disorientation or unconsciousness.
3. Septum: A strike to this area can result in extreme pain, bleeding and disorientation.
4. Front teeth: A strike to this area can result in broken bones and disorientation.
5. Side of jaw: A strike to this area can result in broken bones.
6. Carotid artery: A strike to this area can result in unconsciousness.
7. Larynx: A strike to this area can result in broken bones, permanent damage to the voice or death.
8. Clavicle: A strike to this area can result in broken bones and disabling of the arm.
9. Solar plexus: A strike to this area can disrupt breathing or cause unconsciousness.
10. Floating ribs: A strike to this area can disrupt breathing and result in broken bones, internal injuries and death.
11. Radius bone: A strike to this area can result in numbness to the hand or broken bones.
12. Groin: A strike to this area can result in incapacitating pain, reproductive organ damage (in men) or unconsciousness (in men).
13. Inner thigh: A strike to this area can result in muscle cramping or numbing of the lower leg.
14. Knee: A strike to this area can result in dislocated bones.
15. Instep: A strike to this area can result in dislocated bones.

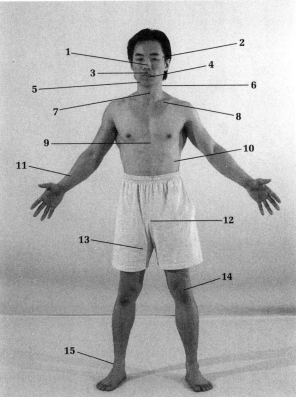

Rear of Body

16. Base of skull: A strike to this area can result in disorientation or unconsciousness.
17. Fourth cervical vertebra: A strike to this area can result in broken bones, paralysis or death.
18. Third lumbar vertebra: A strike to this area can result in broken bones and paralysis.
19. Kidney: A strike to this area can result in internal injuries and death.
20. Coccyx: A strike to this area can result in broken bones and numbness to the legs.
21. Back of knee: A strike to this area can bend the knee or result in dislocated bones.

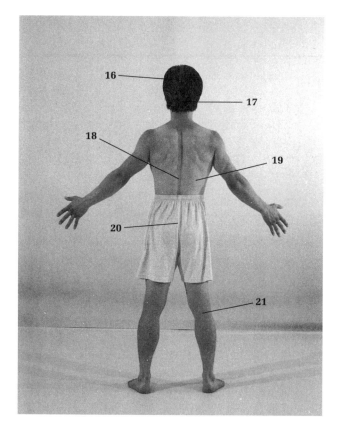

4 Forms

Forms, or formal exercises, are the primary means by which Tae Kwon Do practitioners develop proper technique. Whether the student is a white belt or a senior grand master, all Tae Kwon Do practitioners have forms associated with their belt level. As practitioners rise through the ranks, their forms reflect more and more sophisticated techniques. For black belt practitioners, forms help develop advanced skills such as multiple kicking, simultaneous techniques and ultimately the ability to channel internal power—life force energy.

Unlike the Tae Geuk (eternal vastness) series of forms that Tae Kwon Do students learn at the color belt levels, each of the black belt forms has its own distinct meaning. Each black belt form also follows a unique movement pattern. We have broken each form down into individual movements to show the overall pattern of each one. Because each form follows a different pattern, you should pay close attention to the line and arrow diagrams beside the photographs. The diagrams explain the orientation of the person doing the movements and in which direction he or she is moving. The starting position will always be located at A and move along the lines toward the letters indicated. To keep things as clear as possible, we will always show the forms from the same camera angle except in situations where the person would be facing away from the camera. In those cases, a second photo from the front will accompany the one taken from the normal camera angle so that details of the movement can be seen.

KORYO (KOREA)

The name *Korea* is an adaptation of the name *Koryo,* one of the early dynasties in Korean history (A.D. 918–1392), which is famed for its cultural achievements. In particular, it is during this dynasty that the valiant fighting spirit of its people allowed them to halt the Mongolian invasion of the Korean peninsula. Each movement of the form should be performed with strong conviction to reflect the indomitable spirit and moral determination of the Korean people.

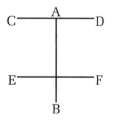

Ready: While standing at A and facing B, slowly raise both hands until they are positioned in front of the face as shown. The motion should be slow and deliberate as if strongly grabbing a large pole with the hands and pushing it away.

Meaning: concentrating energy into the hands.

Movement 1: Turn 90° left toward D in a left back stance and execute a double knife-hand block.

Meaning: defense against an attack to the middle section.

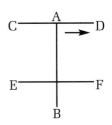

Movement 2a: Pivot on the left foot to execute a low side kick toward D with the right foot.

Meaning: counterattacking kick to the knee.

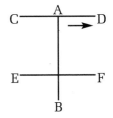

Movement 2b: Execute a middle target kick with the right foot toward D without returning the foot to the floor.

Meaning: second counterattack.

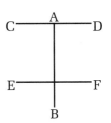

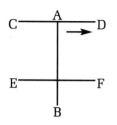

Movement 2c: Step down into a right forward stance facing D and execute an outside knife-hand attack to the neck.

Meaning: third counterattack.

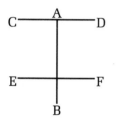

Movement 3: Remain in stance and execute a left reverse punch toward D to middle target.

Meaning: finishing counterattack.

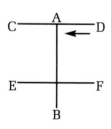

Movement 4: Slide right foot back to a right back stance and execute an inner arm block with the right arm.

Meaning: defense against an attack to the middle section.

Movement 5: Turn 180° right toward C into a right back stance and execute a double knife-hand block.

Meaning: defense against an attack to the middle section

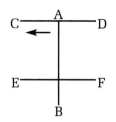

Movement 6a: Pivot on right foot and execute a low side kick toward C with the left foot.

Meaning: counterattacking kick to the knee.

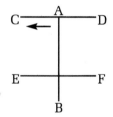

Movement 6b: Execute a middle target kick toward C with the left foot without returning the foot to the floor.

Meaning: second counterattack.

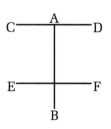

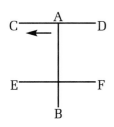

Movement 6c: Step down with left foot into a left forward stance facing C and execute an outside knife-hand strike to the neck.

Meaning: third counterattack.

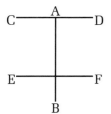

Movement 7: Remain in the same stance and execute a middle target punch with the right hand toward C.

Meaning: finishing counterattack.

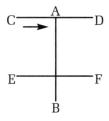

Movement 8: Slide left foot back into a back stance facing C and execute an inner arm block with the left hand.

Meaning: defense against an attack to the middle section.

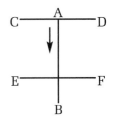

Movement 9a: Turn 90° left into a forward stance facing B and execute a knife-hand down block with the left hand.

Meaning: defense against an attack to the low section.

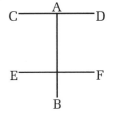

Movement 9b: Remain in the same stance and execute an arc-hand attack to the throat toward B with the right hand.

Meaning: lethal counterattack.

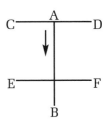

Movement 10a: Execute a middle target front kick toward B with the right foot.

Meaning: counterattack.

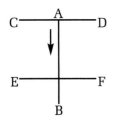

Movement 10b: Step down with right foot into a right forward stance facing B and execute a knife-hand down block with the right hand.

Meaning: defense against an attack to the lower section.

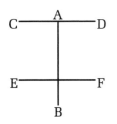

Movement 10c: Remain in the same stance and execute an arc-hand attack to the throat toward B with the left hand.

Meaning: lethal counterattack.

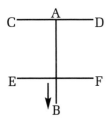

Movement 11a: Execute a middle target kick toward B with the left foot.

Meaning: counterattack.

Movement 11b: Step down with left foot into a left forward stance facing B and execute a knife-hand down block with the left hand.

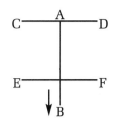

Movement 11c: Remain in the same stance and execute an arc-hand attack to the throat with the right hand toward B. Yell "*Ki-hop!*"

Meaning: lethal counterattack.

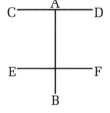

Movement 12a: Execute a middle target front kick toward B with the right foot.

Meaning: counterattack.

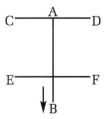

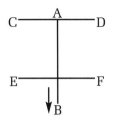

Movement 12b: Step down with the right foot into a right forward stance facing B. At the same time, sweep the right hand across the front of the body until the forearm is parallel to the floor while executing a downward arc-hand strike toward B with the left hand.

Meaning: Capture the opponent's kicking foot with the right hand and dislocate the knee backward.

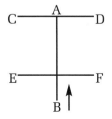

Movement 13: Turn 180° right into a right forward stance facing A and execute double outer arm block with both arms.

Meaning: blocking a double attack to the middle section.

Movement 14a: Execute a middle target front kick toward A with the left foot.

Meaning: counterattack.

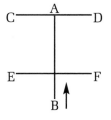

Movement 14b: Step down with left foot into a left forward stance facing A. Sweep left arm across front of body until forearm is parallel to the floor and execute a downward arc-hand strike toward A with the right hand.

Meaning: Capture the opponent's kicking foot with the left hand and dislocate the knee backward.

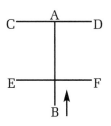

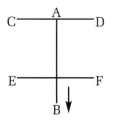

Movement 15: Draw back the left foot into a left walking stance facing A and execute double outer arm blocks.

Meaning: defense against a double attack to the middle section.

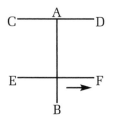

Movement 16: Turn 270° left into a horseback riding stance facing F and execute a single knife-hand block toward F with the left hand.

Meaning: defense against an attack to the high section.

Movement 17: Remain in stance and flex left wrist so that palm is turned in and strike palm with right fist.

Meaning: Grasp the opponent by the back of head and counterattack.

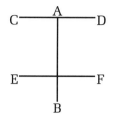

Movement 18a: Step into twist stance by crossing right leg in front of left.

Meaning: preparation for side kick.

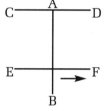

Movement 18b: Execute a middle target side kick toward F with left foot.

Meaning: finishing counterattack.

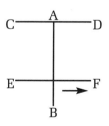

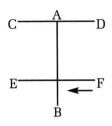

Movement 18c: Step down with left foot and twist 180° right into a right forward stance facing E while executing a palm up spear-fingers attack to the groin.

Meaning: preemptive counterattack.

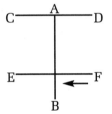

Movement 19: Slide left foot forward into a right walking stance facing E while executing a down block with the right arm.

Meaning: defense against an attack to the lower section.

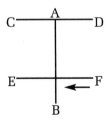

Movement 20a: Step forward with left foot into a left walking stance facing E and execute an inner palm block with the left hand.

Meaning: defense against an attack to the middle section.

Movement 20b: Twist trunk and execute an inner elbow strike to the jaw.
Meaning: counterattack.

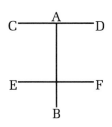

Movement 20c: Step forward with right foot into a horse back riding stance facing E and execute a supported outer elbow strike to the middle target wih the right elbow.

Meaning: finishing counterattack.

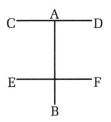

Movement 21: Remain in stance and execute a single knife-hand block toward E with the right hand.

Meaning: defense against an attack to the upper section.

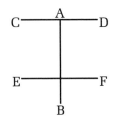

Movement 22: Remain in stance and flex right wrist so that palm faces in and strike palm with left fist.

Meaning: Counterattack to face by holding opponent by the back of the neck and punching.

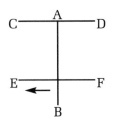

Movement 23a: Step into twist stance by crossing left foot in front of right.

Meaning: preparation for side kick.

Movement 23b: Execute a right side kick to middle target toward E.

Meaning: finishing counterattack.

Movement 23c: Step down with right foot and turn 180° left into a left forward stance facing F and execute a palm up spear-fingers strike to the groin.

Meaning: preemptive counterattack.

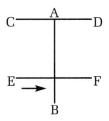

Movement 24: Slide right foot forward into a left walking stance facing F and execute a down block with the left arm.

Meaning: defense against an attack to the lower section.

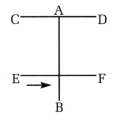

Movement 25a: Step forward with right foot into a right walking stance facing F and execute an inner palm block with the right hand.

Meaning: defense against an attack to the middle section.

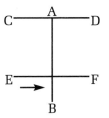

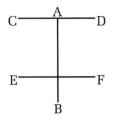

Movement 25b: Twist trunk and execute an inner elbow strike to the jaw.

Meaning: counterattack.

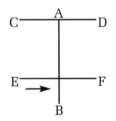

Movement 25c: Step forward with left foot into a horseback riding stance facing F and execute a supported outer elbow strike to the middle target with the left elbow.

Meaning: finishing counterattack.

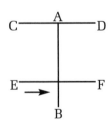

Movement 26a: Draw left foot to the right one and face B in an upright stance while bringing hands above head with the left hand in a fist and right hand open as shown.

Meaning: concentrating energy into the hands.

Movement 26b: Remain in stance and circle hands slowly down in wide arcs. When hands are six inches apart, bring them together quickly to strike open palm of right hand with left hammer-fist.

Meaning: finishing counterattack by taking forehead of collapsing opponent in palm and striking the back of the head.

Movement 27a: Turn 180° left into a left forward stance facing A and execute an outer knife-hand attack to the neck with the left hand.

Meaning: preemptive counterattack.

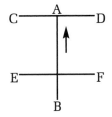

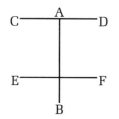

Movement 27b: Remain in stance and execute a knife-hand down block with the left hand.

Meaning: defense against an attack to the lower section.

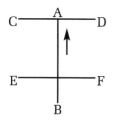

Movement 28a: Step forward with the right foot into a right forward stance facing A and execute an inner knife-hand strike to the neck with the right hand.

Meaning: counterattack.

Movement 28b: Remain in stance and execute a knife-hand down block with the right hand.

Meaning: defense against an attack to the low section.

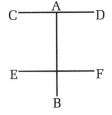

Movement 29a: Step forward with left foot into a left forward stance facing A and execute an inner knife-hand attack to the neck with the left hand.

Meaning: counterattack.

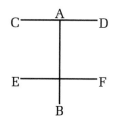

Movement 29b: Remain in stance and execute a knife-hand down block with the left hand.

Meaning: defense against an attack to the lower section.

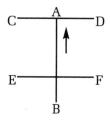

Movement 30: Step forward with the right foot into a right forward stance facing A and execute an arc-hand attack to the throat with the right hand. Yell, "*Ki-hop!*"

Meaning: lethal counterattack.

Ready: Turn 180° left to face B in an upright stance. Bring both hands slowly up before face as shown as if grabbing a large pole and pushing it away.

Meaning: concentrating energy into the hands.

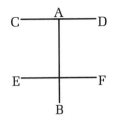

KUMKANG (DIAMOND)

The original meaning of *Kumkang* is "too strong to be broken." In Buddhism it also refers to something that can heal mental anguish through a combination of wisdom and virtue. In Korea, the most beautiful mountain in the Taebek mountain range is called Kumkang. The "diamond" form takes its name from Mount Kumkang and reflects all of the virtues associated with it as a symbol of solidity and permanence. The movements of this form should be performed powerfully to represent the immovable majesty of the mountain.

Ready: The normal *joonbi* stance is the ready stance for this form.

Meaning: preparing the mind and body for action.

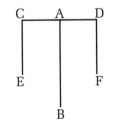

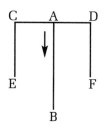

Movement 1: Step forward with the left foot into a left forward stance facing B and execute double outer arm blocks.

Meaning: defense against a double attack to the middle section.

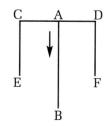

Movement 2: Step forward with the right foot into a right forward stance facing B and execute a palm strike to the face with the right hand.

Meaning: counterattack.

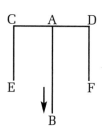

Movement 3: Step forward with the left foot into a left forward stance facing B and execute a palm strike to the face using the left hand.

Meaning: second counterattack.

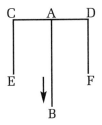

Movement 4: Step forward with the right foot into a right forward stance facing B and execute a palm strike to the face with the right hand.

Meaning: third counterattack.

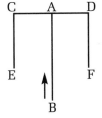

Movement 5: Step back with the right foot into a left back stance facing B and execute an inner knife-hand block with the left hand.

Meaning: defense against an attack to the upper section.

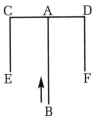

Movement 6: Step back with the left foot into a right back stance facing B and execute an inner knife-hand block with the right hand.

Meaning: defense against an attack to the upper section.

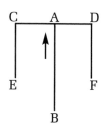

Movement 7: Step back with the right foot into a left back stance facing B and execute an inner knife-hand block with the left hand.

Meaning: defense against an attack to the upper section.

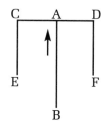

Movement 8: Shift all weight back to the right foot and execute a diamond block facing left as illustrated.

Meaning: defense against simultaneous attacks to the upper and lower sections.

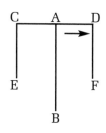

Movement 9: Step out to the left with the left foot into a horseback riding stance facing D and execute a simultaneous hook punch with the right fist and backward elbow strike with the left elbow.

Meaning: double counterattack.

Movement 10a: Step across the left foot and spin 360°.

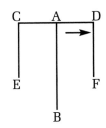

Movement 10b: Step down from spin with left foot into a horseback riding stance facing D and execute a simultaneous hook punch with the right fist and backward elbow strike with the left elbow.

Meaning: double counterattack.

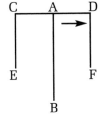

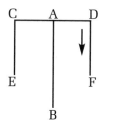

Movement 11: Step toward F with the right foot into a horseback riding stance and execute a mountain block. Yell, "*Ki-hop!*"

Meaning: defense against simultaneous attacks to the upper section from opposite directions.

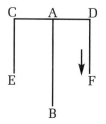

Movement 12: Step toward F with the left foot into a horseback riding stance and execute simultaneous outer arm blocks.

Meaning: defense against simultaneous attacks to the middle section.

Movement 13: Slowly slide the left foot back toward the right until feet are shoulder width apart and stand in an upright position. At the same time, fists are brought down and to the side in slow down blocks to the outside. The entire movement should take five seconds.

Meaning: powerful double defense against simultaneous attacks to the lower section from opposite sides.

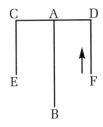

Movement 14: Step toward D with the right foot into a horseback riding stance and execute a mountain block.

Meaning: defense against simultaneous attacks to the high section from opposite sides.

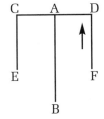

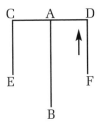

Movement 15: Shift weight to the left foot and spin 270° right and execute a diamond block facing C as illustrated.

Meaning: defense against simultaneous attacks to the upper and lower sections.

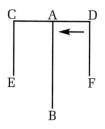

Movement 16: Step out with the right foot toward C into a horseback riding stance facing C and execute a simultaneous hook punch with the left fist and backward elbow strike with the right elbow.

Meaning: double counterattack.

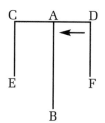

Movement 17a: Step across the right foot and spin 360°.

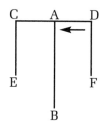

Movement 17b: Step down toward C with the right foot into a horseback riding stance facing C and execute a simultaneous hook punch with the left fist and a backward elbow strike with the right elbow.

Meaning: double counterattack.

Movement 18: Shift weight back to the left foot and execute a diamond block facing C as illustrated.

Meaning: defense against simultaneous attacks to the upper and lower sections.

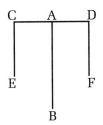

Movement 19: Step down toward C with the right foot into a horseback riding stance facing C and execute a simultaneous hook punch with the left fist and a backward elbow strike with the right elbow.

Meaning: double counterattack.

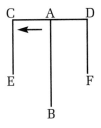

Movement 20a: Step across the right foot and spin 360°.

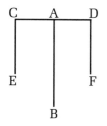

Movement 20b: Step down from spin toward C with the right foot into a horseback riding stance and execute a simultaneous hook punch with the left fist and a backward elbow strike with the left elbow.

Meaning: double counterattack.

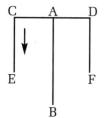

Movement 21: Step toward E with the left foot into a horseback riding stance and execute a mountain block. Yell, "*Ki-hop!*"

Meaning: defense against simultaneous attacks to the upper section.

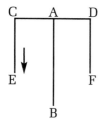

Movement 22: Step toward E with the right foot into a horseback riding stance and execute two outer arm blocks.

Meaning: defense against simultaneous attacks to the middle section.

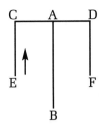

Movement 23: Slowly slide the right foot back toward the left until feet are shoulder width apart and stand in an upright position. At the same time, fists are brought down and to the side in slow motion down blocks to the outside. The entire movement should take five seconds.

Meaning: powerful double defense against simultaneous attacks to the lower section from opposite sides.

Movement 24: Step toward C with the right foot into a horseback riding stance and execute a mountain block.

Meaning: defense against simultaneous attacks to the high section from opposite directions.

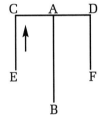

Movement 25: Shift weight to the right foot and spin 270° right and execute a diamond block facing left as illustrated.

Meaning: defense against simultaneous attacks to the upper and lower sections.

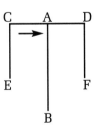

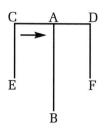

Movement 26: Step down toward A with the right foot into a horseback riding stance facing A and execute a simultaneous hook punch with the right fist and a backward elbow strike with the left elbow.

Meaning: simultaneous counterattack.

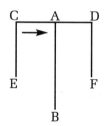

Movement 27a: Step across right foot and spin 360°.

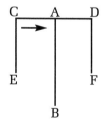

Movement 27b: Step down from spin with left foot toward A into a horseback riding stance and execute a simultaneous hook punch with the right fist and a backward elbow strike with the left elbow.

Meaning: double counterattack.

Ready: *joonbi* stance.

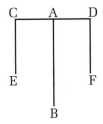

TAEBEK (SACRED MOUNTAIN)

Taebek is the ancient name of the modern day Mount Paekdoo, the highest and grandest mountain in Korea. Legends identify this as the place where the semi-divine being Tan-gun founded the kingdom of Choson 4,300 years ago and established the beginning of the Korean nation. Mount Paekdoo is regarded as the symbol of Korea. The movements of this form should be performed with precision and rigorous dexterity as a sign of respect for cultural heritage.

Ready: *joonbi* stance.

Meaning: preparing the body and mind for action.

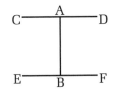

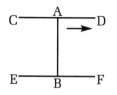

Movement 1: From A, turn 90° left and assume a left tiger stance facing D while executing low knife-hand blocks with both hands.

Meaning: defense against simultaneous attacks to the low section.

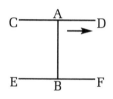

Movement 2a: Execute a middle target front kick toward D with the right foot.

Meaning: counterattack.

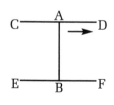

Movement 2b: Step down with right foot into a right forward stance facing D and execute a middle target punch with the right hand.

Meaning: second counterattack

Movement 2c: Remain in stance and execute a middle target punch with the left hand.

Meaning: finishing counterattack.

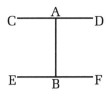

Movement 3: Pivot 180° right on left foot into a right tiger stance facing C and execute low knife-hand blocks with both hands.

Meaning: defense against simultaneous attacks to the low section.

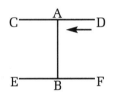

Movement 4a: Execute a middle target front kick toward C with the left foot.

Meaning: counterattack.

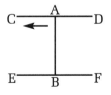

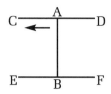

Movement 4b: Step down with the left foot into a left forward stance facing C and execute a middle target punch with the left hand.

Meaning: second counterattack.

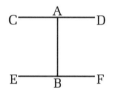

Movement 4c: Remain in stance and execute a middle target punch toward C with the right hand.

Meaning: finishing counterattack.

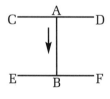

Movement 5: Step 90° left with the left foot into a left forward stance facing B and execute a simultaneous knife-hand rising block with the left hand and a knife-hand strike to the neck with the right hand.

Meaning: simultaneous defense against an attack to the upper section and counterattack.

Movement 6: Turn right hand palm down and close fingers into a fist, then step forward with the right foot into a right forward stance facing B and execute a middle target punch with the left fist.

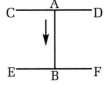

Meaning: grabbing the opponent's wrist and counterattacking.

Movement 7: Turn left hand palm down and close fingers into a fist, then step forward with the left foot into a left forward stance facing B and execute a middle target punch with the right fist.

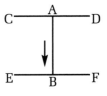

Meaning: grabbing the opponent's wrist and counterattacking.

Movement 8: Turn right hand palm down and close fingers into a fist, then step forward with the right foot into a right forward stance facing B and execute a middle target punch with the left fist. Yell, "*Ki-hop!*"

Meaning: grabbing the opponent's wrist and counterattacking.

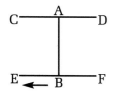

Movement 9: Turn 270° left into a left back stance facing E and execute a simultaneous rising block and outer arm block.

Meaning: defense against simultaneous attacks to the upper section from different directions.

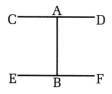

Movement 10: Remain in stance and pull left fist to right shoulder while executing a strong uppercut punch to the chin with the right fist.

Meaning: grabbing and pulling the opponent's clothes to counterattack.

Movement 11: Remain in stance and execute a middle section punch with the left hand.

Meaning: counterattack.

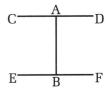

Movement 12: Shift weight to right foot and raise left foot while bringing both fists to the right hip.

Meaning: concentrating energy in preparation to kick.

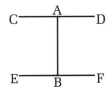

Movement 13a: Execute a middle section side kick with the left foot toward E.

Meaning: third counterattack.

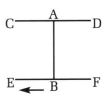

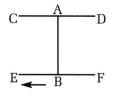

Movement 13b: Step down with the left foot into a left forward stance facing E and execute an elbow strike with the right elbow to the right palm.

Meaning: holding the opponent by the back of the head to deliver a finishing counterattack.

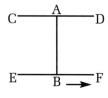

Movement 14: Turn 180° right into a right back stance facing F and execute a simultaneous rising block with the left arm and outer arm block with the right hand.

Meaning: defense against simultaneous attacks to the upper section from different directions.

Movement 15: Remain in stance and pull right fist to left shoulder while executing an uppercut punch to the jaw toward F with the left fist.

Meaning: grabbing and pulling the opponent's clothes to counterattack.

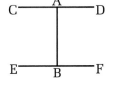

Movement 16: Remain in stance and execute a middle section punch with the right hand.

Meaning: second counterattack.

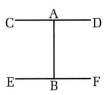

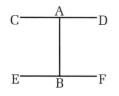

Movement 17: Shift weight onto the left foot and raise the right foot while bringing both fists to the left hip.

Meaning: concentrating energy in preparation to kick.

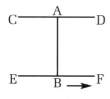

Movement 18a: Execute a middle target side kick toward F with the right foot.

Meaning: third counterattack.

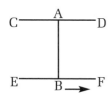

Movement 18b: Step down with right foot into a right forward stance facing F and execute an elbow strike with the left elbow to the right palm.

Meaning: holding the opponent by the back of the head to deliver a finishing counterattack.

Movement 19: Step toward A with the left foot into a left back stance and execute a double knife-hand block.

Meaning: defense against an attack to the middle section.

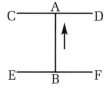

Movement 20: Step forward with the right foot into a right forward stance facing A. Execute an inner palm block with the left hand and a spear-fingers attack to middle target with the right hand.

Meaning: simultaneous defense against an attack to the middle section and counterattack.

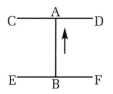

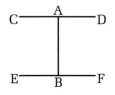

Movement 21a: While keeping the feet in the same places on the floor, twist the right shoulder so that the trunk turns 180° so that you are facing B with the left leg bent and the right leg straight. The left forearm remains across the body while the right arm twists to point the elbow up.

Meaning: pulling the right wrist free of the opponent's grip.

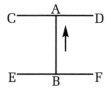

Movement 21b: Pivot 180° left on right foot and step toward A with the left foot into a left back stance. Execute a back-fist strike to the head with the left hand.

Meaning: counterattack.

Movement 22: Step forward with the right foot into a right forward stance facing A and execute a middle target punch with the right fist. Yell, *"Ki-hop!"*

Meaning: finishing counterattack.

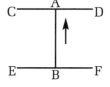

Movement 23: Pivot 270° left on the right foot and step out with the left foot into a left forward stance facing D. Execute a scissors block—right hand up and left hand down.

Meaning: defense against a double attack to the middle section.

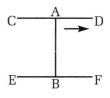

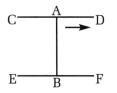

Movement 24a: Execute a middle target front kick toward D with the right foot.

Meaning: counterattack.

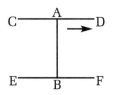

Movement 24b: Step down with the right foot into a right forward stance facing D and execute a middle target punch with the right fist.

Meaning: second counterattack.

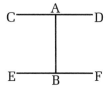

Movement 24c: Remain in stance and execute a middle target punch with the left hand.

Meaning: third counterattack.

Movement 25: Turn 180° right with the right foot into a right forward stance facing C and execute a scissors block—left arm up and right arm down.

Meaning: defense against a double attack to the middle section.

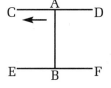

Movement 26a: Execute a middle target front kick toward C with the left foot.

Meaning: counterattack.

Movement 26b: Step down with the left foot into a left front stance facing C and execute a middle target punch with the left hand.

Meaning: second counterattack.

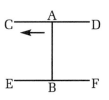

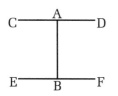

Movement 26c: Remain in stance and execute a middle section punch toward C with the right hand.

Meaning: third counterattack.

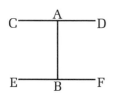

Ready: *joonbi.*

PYUNG WON (VAST PLAIN)

The fertile plains are where humans obtain sustenance. It is also the place where we conduct our lives. A vast, open plain that stretches away in all directions imparts a feeling of majesty and life. It is this feeling of abundance and boundlessness that is the foundation of this form. The movements of this form should be done with a reserved grace to reflect this concept.

Ready: Stand at attention with the hands held open flat and placed right over left as illustrated.

Meaning: making the hands hard with energy.

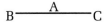

Movement 1: Step out with left foot until feet are shoulder width apart. Hands are separated and brought very slowly out to the sides in knife-hand blocks. The movement should take five seconds.

Meaning: strong defense against an attack to the lower section

Movement 2: Remain in stance and slowly bring palms together and slowly push up before face as if grabbing a heavy pole and pushing it away.

Meaning: forcing the opponent's choking hands away.

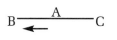

Movement 3: Step toward B with right foot into a right back stance and execute a low knife-hand block.

Meaning: defense against an attack to the low section.

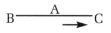

Movement 4: Turn 180° left into a back stance facing C and execute an outer knife-hand block.

Meaning: defense against an attack to the middle section.

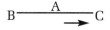

Movement 5: Step out with left foot toward C into a left forward stance and execute an upward elbow strike with the right elbow to the chin.

Meaning: counterattack.

Movement 6a: Execute a front kick toward C with the right foot.

Meaning: second counterattack.

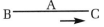

Movement 6b: Step down with right foot and spin left.

Movement 6c: Execute a spinning back kick toward C with the left foot.

Meaning: finishing counterattack.

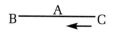

Movement 6d: Step down with left foot and turn to face B in a right back stance. Execute a double knife-hand block.

Meaning: defense against an attack to the middle section.

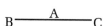

Movement 7: Remain in stance and execute a low double knife-hand block. Both hands should make large circles up to the rear and down.

Meaning: defense against an attack to the low section.

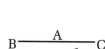

Movement 8: Step out with the right foot toward B into a horseback riding stance and execute an outer arm block with the right arm as the left arm covers the body.

Meaning: defense against an attack to the high section with additional body protection.

Movement 9a: Pick up the right foot and swing the right arm back,

B———A———C

Movement 9b: Stamp down with right foot into a horseback riding stance with head facing forward and execute an inner arm block with the right arm as the left arm covers the body.

Meaning: defense against an attack to the high section with additional body protection.

B———A——←—C

Movement 9c: Remain in stance and execute an inner arm block with the left arm as the right arm covers the body. Yell, "*Ki-hop!*"

Meaning: defense against an attack to the high section with additional body protection.

B———A———C

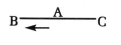

Movement 10: Step the left foot across the right into a twist stance facing B and execute simultaneous outward elbow strikes.

Meaning: simultaneous counterattack against two opponents.

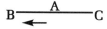

Movement 11: Step out with right foot toward B into a horseback riding stance and execute a mountain block.

Meaning: counterattack against simultaneous attacks to the high section from opposite directions.

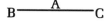

Movement 12a: Shift weight to the left foot and execute a diamond block facing B as illustrated.

Meaning: defense against simultaneous attacks to the upper and lower sections.

Movement 12b: Remain in stance and bring both fists to the left hip.

Meaning: concentrating power in preparation for a kick.

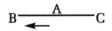

Movement 13a: Execute a side kick toward B with the right foot.

Meaning: counterattack.

Movement 13b: Step down with right foot into a forward stance facing B and execute an upward elbow strike to the jaw with the left elbow.

Meaning: second counterattack.

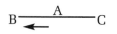

Movement 14a: Execute a front kick toward B with the left foot.

Meaning: third counterattack.

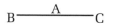

Movement 14b: Step down with the left foot and spin left,

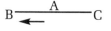

Movement 14c: Execute a spinning back kick toward B with the right foot.

Meaning: finishing counterattack.

Movement 14d: Step down with right foot and turn 180° into a left back stance facing C. Execute a double knife-hand block.

Meaning: defense against an attack to the middle section.

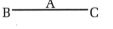

Movement 15: Remain in stance and execute a low double knife-hand block. Both hands should make large circles up to the rear and down.

Meaning: defense against an attack to the lower section.

Movement 16: Step out with left foot toward C into a horseback riding stance and execute an outer arm block with the left arm while the right arm covers the body.

Meaning: defense against an attack to the high section with additional body protection.

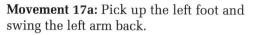

Movement 17a: Pick up the left foot and swing the left arm back.

Movement 17b: Stamp down with the right foot into a horseback riding stance with the head facing forward. Execute an inner arm block with the left arm while the right arm covers the body.

Meaning: defense against an attack to the high section with additional body protection.

Movement 17c: Execute an inner arm block with the right arm while the left arm covers the body. Yell, "*Ki-hop!*"

Meaning: defense against an attack to the high section with additional body protection.

Movement 18: Cross the right leg over the left into a twist stance facing C and execute simultaneous outward elbow strikes.

Meaning: counterattack against two opponents.

B———A———C
→

Movement 19: Step out with left foot toward C into a horseback riding stance and execute a mountain block.

Meaning: defense against simultaneous attacks to the upper section from opposite directions.

B———A———C
→

Movement 20a: Shift weight to the right foot and execute a diamond block facing C as illustrated.

Meaning: defense against simultaneous attacks to the upper and lower sections.

B———A———C

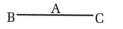

Movement 20b: Remain in stance and bring both fists to the right hip.

Meaning: concentrating power in preparation to deliver a kick.

Movement 21a: Execute a side kick toward C with the left foot.

Meaning: counterattack.

Movement 21b: Step down with the left foot into a left forward stance facing C and execute an elbow strike toward C with the right elbow into the palm of the left hand.

Meaning: Hold opponent by the back of the head to deliver a finishing counterattack.

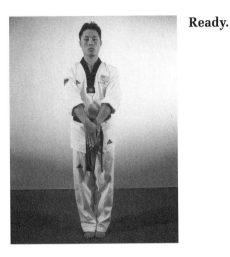

Ready.

B ———A——— C

SHIP JIN (SYMMETRY)

The literal meaning of *ship jin* is "decimal system." It represents endless growth and development in a balanced, systematic order. Through this form, stability and balance are strived for. The movements of this form should be performed with precision and control.

Ready: *joonbi* stance.

Meaning: preparing the mind and body for action.

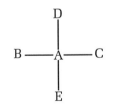

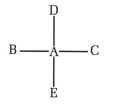

Movement 1: Keep feet in place and raise both arms slowly to execute powerful, simultaneous rising blocks.

Meaning: defense against two simultaneous attacks to the high section.

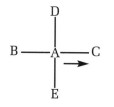

Movement 2: Step 90° left with left foot into a left back stance facing C and execute an outer arm block with the left hand supported by the right palm as shown.

Meaning: strong defense against an attack to the high section.

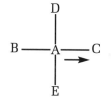

Movement 3a: Open left hand and turn it palm down, making a grasping motion. Slide the left foot forward into a left forward stance facing C and execute a palm down spear-fingers attack to middle target with the right hand.

Meaning: grab opponent's wrist and counterattack.

Movement 3b: Remain in stance and execute a middle target punch toward C with the left fist.

Meaning: second counterattack.

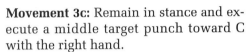

Movement 3c: Remain in stance and execute a middle target punch toward C with the right hand.

Meaning: third counterattack.

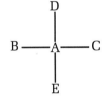

Movement 4: Step toward C with right foot into a horseback riding stance facing C and execute a mountain block.

Meaning: defense against simultaneous attacks to the high section from opposite directions.

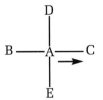

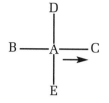

Movement 5a: Step across right foot into a twist stance facing C as right fist pulls back to chamber and left hand crosses in front of chest making a grasping motion.

Meaning: stepping close to opponent and grabbing the wrist of his punching hand.

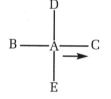

Movement 5b: Step out with right fist toward C into a horseback riding stance facing C and execute a middle section side punch with the right fist as left hand pulls back to chamber. Yell, "*Ki-hop!*"

Meaning: pulling the opponent close to deliver a finishing blow.

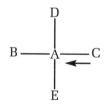

Movement 6: Turn 180° right and step toward B with the right foot into a horseback riding stance facing B. Execute simultaneous outward elbow strikes to middle target.

Meaning: double counterattack to opponents on opposite sides.

Movement 7: Pivot right foot toward B and adopt a right back stance facing B. Execute an outer arm block with the right arm supported by the left palm as shown.

Meaning: strong defense against an attack to the high section.

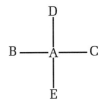

Movement 8a: Open right hand and turn it palm down, making a grasping motion. Slide right foot forward toward B into a forward stance facing B and execute a palm down spear-fingers strike to middle target.

Meaning: grab opponent's wrist and counterattack.

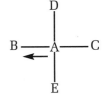

Movement 8b: Remain in stance and execute a middle target punch toward B with the right hand.

Meaning: second counterattack.

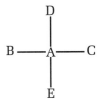

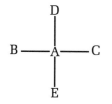

Movement 8c: Remain in stance and execute a middle target punch toward B with the left hand.

Meaning: third counterattack.

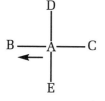

Movement 9: Step toward B with the right foot into a horseback riding stance facing B and execute a mountain block.

Meaning: defense against simultaneous attacks to the high section from opposite sides.

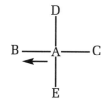

Movement 10a: Step across left foot into a twist stance facing B as left fist pulls back to chamber and right hand crosses in front of chest making a grasping motion.

Meaning: stepping close to opponent and grabbing the wrist of his punching hand.

Movement 10b: Step out with the left foot toward B into a horseback riding stance facing B and execute a middle target side punch with the left hand as the right hand pulls back to chamber. Yell, "*Ki-hop!*"

Meaning: pulling the opponent close to deliver a finishing blow.

```
          D
          |
  B ——— A ——— C
   ←
          |
          E
```

Movement 11: Turn 180° left and step out with left foot into a horseback riding stance facing C and execute simultaneous outward elbow strikes to middle target.

Meaning: double counterattack.

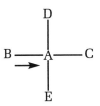

```
          D
          |
  B ——— A ——— C
   →
          |
          E
```

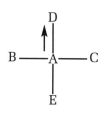

Movement 12: Turn 90° right and step out with right foot into a right back stance facing D. Execute an outer arm block with the right arm supported with the left palm.

Meaning: strong defense against an attack to the high section.

Movement 13a: Slide right foot forward into a forward stance facing D and turn the right hand palm down while making a grasping motion. Execute a palm down spear-fingers strike toward D with the left hand as the right hand draws back to chamber.

Meaning: Pull opponent close to counterattack.

Movement 13b: Remain in stance and execute a middle target punch toward D with the right hand.

Meaning: second counterattack.

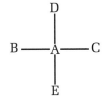

Movement 13c: Remain in stance and execute a middle target punch toward D with the left hand.

Meaning: third counterattack.

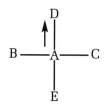

Movement 14: Step toward D into a back stance and execute a middle target punch toward D with the left hand while the right arm protects the middle section.

Meaning: counterattack.

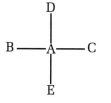

Movement 15a: Remain in stance and bring both open hands to the right hip.

Meaning: concentrating energy into the hands and arms to strengthen them.

Movement 15b: Remain in stance and slowly raise hands up and forward in a powerful pushing motion as if pushing a large rock away.

Meaning: strong defense against an attack to the high section.

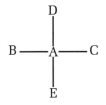

Movement 16: Pivot 90° left on right foot as left foot slides back into a horseback riding stance. Execute simultaneous outer arm block with hands held in palm up knife-hands.

Meaning: defense against a double attack to the middle section.

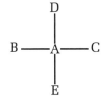

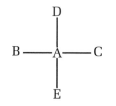

Movement 17: Remain in stance and execute simultaneous low knife-hand blocks to both sides.

Meaning: defense against simultaneous attacks to the low section from opposite sides.

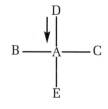

Movement 18: Keep feet in place and slowly straighten knees until standing upright as hands close into fists.

Meaning: concentrating energy in the body in preparation for action.

Movement 19: Turn 90° left into a left forward stance facing E. Sweep left forearm upward in front of the body until the forearm is parallel to the floor as shown.

Meaning: Capture the opponent's kicking foot.

Movement 20a: Remain in stance and bring open hands to right hip.

Meaning: concentrating energy into the hands and arms.

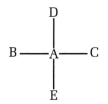

Movement 20b: Remain in stance and slowly raise hands up and forward in a powerful pushing motion as if pushing a large rock away.

Meaning: strong defense against an attack to the high section.

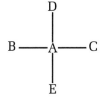

Movement 21a: Remain in stance and bring both fists to the left hip.

Meaning: concentrating energy into the hands.

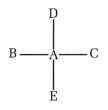

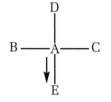

Movement 21b: Execute a front kick toward E with the right foot.

Meaning: counterattack.

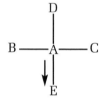

Movement 21c: Step down with the right foot into a forward stance facing E and execute double punches to the middle section.

Meaning: double counterattack.

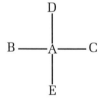

Movement 22a: Remain in stance and draw both fists to right hip.

Meaning: concentrating energy into the hands.

Movement 22b: Execute a front kick toward E with the left foot.

Meaning: counterattack.

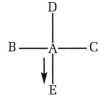

Movement 22c: Step down with the left foot into a left forward stance facing E and execute double punches to the middle section.

Meaning: double counterattack.

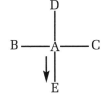

Movement 23a: Remain in stance and draw both fists to the left hip.

Meaning: concentrating energy into the hands and arms.

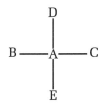

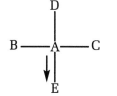

Movement 23b: Execute a front kick toward E with the right foot.

Meaning: counterattack.

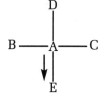

Movement 23c: Hop forward into a right twist stance facing E and execute an outer arm block with the right arm as the left arm guards the middle section. Yell, "*Ki-hop!*"

Meaning: defense against an attack to the high section.

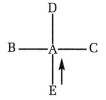

Movement 24a: Turn 180° left into a left forward stance facing D and bring both open hands to the right hip.

Meaning: concentrating energy into the hands and arms.

Movement 24b: Remain in stance and slowly raise hands up and forward in a powerful pushing motion as if pushing a large rock away.

Meaning: strong defense against an attack to the high section.

```
        D
        |
B ——— A ——— C
        |
        E
```

Movement 25: Slide left foot back into a tiger stance facing D and execute a low X block using palm out knife-hands.

Meaning: defense against an attack to the groin.

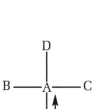

```
        D
        |
B ——— A ——— C
        |↑
        E
```

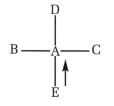

Movement 26: Step forward with the right foot toward D into a right back stance facing D and execute an outer arm block with the right arm as the left arm protects the middle section. Both hands are open in knife-hands—right hand palm up, left hand palm down.

Meaning: defense against an attack to the high section.

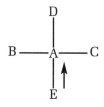

Movement 27: Step forward with the left foot toward D into a left back stance facing D and execute a middle section punch with the left hand as the right arm protects the middle section.

Meaning: counterattack.

Movement 28: Step forward with the right foot toward D into a left back stance facing D and execute a middle target punch with the right hand as the left arm protects the middle section.

Meaning: counterattack.

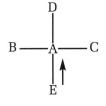

Ready.

Ji Tae (Earth)

All of the living things of the earth have their origins in the earth. In fact, all natural phenomena on our planet originate from changes in the earth. This form reflects the cyclical changes of the earth. The movements of this form should be done with emphasis on solidly rooted stances to represent our connection with the earth.

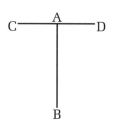

Ready: *joonbi.*

Meaning: preparing the mind and body for action.

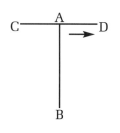

Movement 1: Step toward D with the left foot into a left back stance facing D and execute an outer arm block with the left arm.

Meaning: defense against an attack to the high section.

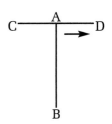

Movement 2a: Step forward with the right foot into a right forward stance facing D and execute a rising block with the right arm.

Meaning: defense against an attack to the high section.

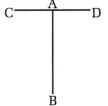

Movement 2b: Remain in stance and execute a middle target punch toward D with the left hand.

Meaning: counterattack.

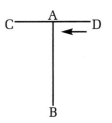

Movement 3: Turn 180° right into a right back stance facing C and execute an outer arm block with the right arm.

Meaning: defense against an attack to the high section.

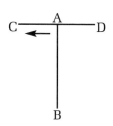

Movement 4a: Step forward with the left foot into a left forward stance facing C and execute a rising block with the left arm.

Meaning: defense against an attack to the high section.

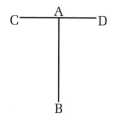

Movement 4b: Remain in stance and execute a middle section punch with the right hand.

Meaning: counterattack.

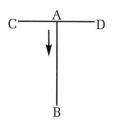

Movement 5: Step 90° right into a right forward stance facing B and execute a down block with the right arm.

Meaning: defense against an attack to the lower section.

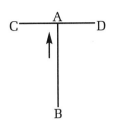

Movement 6: Pivot on right foot and slide left foot back into a left back stance facing B and execute a knife-hand rising block with the left hand.

Meaning: defense against an attack to the high section.

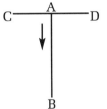

Movement 7a: Execute a front kick toward B with the right foot.

Meaning: counterattack.

Movement 7b: Step down with the right foot into a right back stance facing B and execute a low double knife-hand block.

Meaning: defense against an attack to the low section.

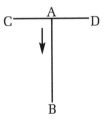

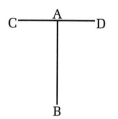

Movement 8: Remain in stance and execute a reverse outer arm block with the right arm.

Meaning: defense against an attack to the high section.

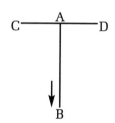

Movement 9a: Execute a front kick toward B with the right foot.

Meaning: counterattack.

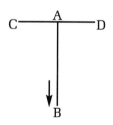

Movement 9b: Step down with the right foot into a right back stance facing B and execute a low double knife-hand block.

Meaning: defense against an attack to the lower section.

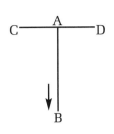

Movement 10: Slide left foot forward into a left forward stance facing B and execute a rising block with the left arm.

Meaning: defense against an attack to the high section

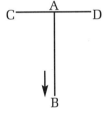

Movement 11: Keep left hand in place and step forward with the right foot into a right forward stance facing B and execute a middle target punch with the right hand.

Meaning: Ward off the opponent's attacking arm and counterattack.

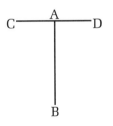

Movement 12a: Remain in stance and execute an inner arm block with the left arm.

Meaning: defense against an attack to the middle section.

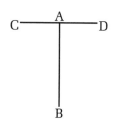

Movement 12b: Remain in stance and execute an inner arm block with the right arm as the left arm protects the middle section.

Meaning: defense against an attack to the upper section.

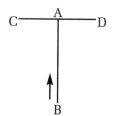

Movement 13: Step back with the right foot into a back stance facing B and execute a low knife-hand block.

Meaning: defense against an attack to the low section.

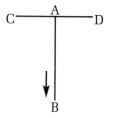

Movement 14a: Execute a front kick toward B with the right foot.

Meaning: counterattack.

Movement 14b: Step down and back with the right foot into a left forward stance facing B and execute a middle target punch with the right hand.

Meaning: second counterattack.

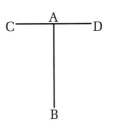

Movement 14c: Remain in stance and execute a middle target punch with the left hand.

Meaning: third counterattack.

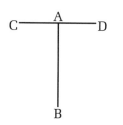

Movement 15: Step back with left foot to turn 90° left into a horseback riding stance with head facing front and execute simultaneous rising blocks.

Meaning: defense against simultaneous attacks to the high section.

Movement 16: Remain in stance and turn the head to look left. Execute a down block to the side with the left arm.

Meaning: defense against an attack to the low section.

Movement 17: Remain in stance and turn head to look right. Execute a single knife-hand block to the side with the right hand.

Meaning: defense against an attack to the high section.

Movement 18: Remain in stance and open the fingers of the right hand and turn the hand palm in. Strike the palm with a left back-fist. Yell, "*Ki-hop!*"

Meaning: Hold opponent by the back of the head to deliver a finishing counter-attack.

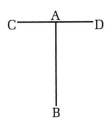

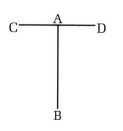

Movement 19: Shift weight to left foot and raise right foot while executing a down block to the outside with the right arm as the left fist pulls back to chamber.

Meaning: defense against an attack to the low section while preparing to kick.

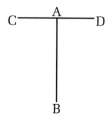

Movement 20: Remain in stance and draw the right fist to the left hip.

Meaning: concentrating energy in the body.

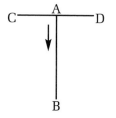

Movement 21a: Execute a side kick toward B with the right foot.

Meaning: counterattack.

Movement 21b: Step down with right foot and raise left foot and execute a down block with the left arm.

Meaning: defense against an attack to the low section while preparing to kick.

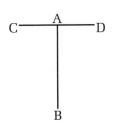

Movement 22: Remain in stance and bring left fist to right hip.

Meaning: concentrating energy in the body.

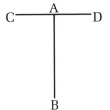

Movement 23a: Execute a side kick toward A with the left foot.

Meaning: counterattack.

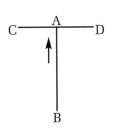

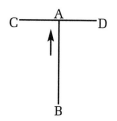

Movement 23b: Step down with the left foot into a left forward stance facing A and execute a middle target punch with the right hand.

Meaning: counterattack.

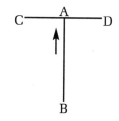

Movement 24: Step forward with the right foot into a right forward stance facing A and execute a middle target punch with the right hand again.

Meaning: second counterattack.

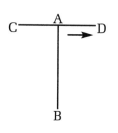

Movement 25: Turn 270° left into a left back stance facing D and execute a low double knife-hand block.

Meaning: defense against an attack to the low section.

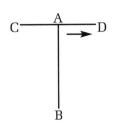

Movement 26: Step forward with the right foot into a right back stance facing D and execute a double knife-hand block.

Meaning: defense against an attack to the middle section.

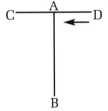

Movement 27: Turn 180° right into a right back stance facing C and execute a low double knife-hand block.

Meaning: defense against an attack to the low section.

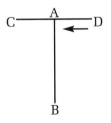

Movement 28: Step forward with the left foot into a left back stance facing C and execute a double knife-hand block.

Meaning: defense against an attack to the middle section.

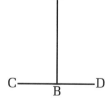

Ready.

Chun Kwon (Sky)

Since very ancient times, the open and mysterious vastness of the sky has made it a source of reverence for people because it was something that could never be reached. Often it was worshipped as the ruler of the universe or the dwelling place of God. This form reflects the profound impact the sky has on the imaginations of humans. The movements of this form should be done with a sense of piety while drawing on internal, life-force energy for power as opposed to physical strength.

Ready: Stand in an upright stance with feet together. Hands are held in knife-hand position low in front of the body with the left hand over the right.

Meaning: concentrating energy into the hands and arms.

Movement 1a: Remain in stance and slowly raise crossed hands along center of body until they are shoulder height with the elbows up to the sides and the fingertips pointing to the opposite shoulders.

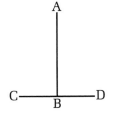

Movement 1b: Remain in stance and flex wrists to point fingers upward as hands are pushed slowly out to both sides until arms are fully extended with palms out. The entire movement should take eight to 10 seconds.

Meaning: generating flowing energy with the arms.

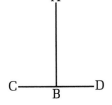

Movement 2a: Remain in stance. While keeping elbows up, slowly circle the hands down and in until they come together before the lower face.

Meaning: slipping the hands between the opponent's arms where he has grabbed the front of the clothes with both hands.

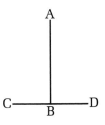

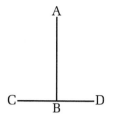

Movement 2b: Remain in stance and turn palms out.

Meaning: defense against a head butt to the face.

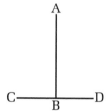

Movement 2c: Remain in stance and slowly circle the hands up and apart, pushing strongly.

Meaning: forcing the opponent to release his grip.

Movement 2d: Step forward with the right foot into a tiger stance facing B and execute simultaneous uppercut knuckle-fist strikes.

Meaning: counterattack.

Movement 3: Slide the right foot forward slightly into a right forward stance facing B and execute a knife-hand block with the left hand.

Meaning: defense against an attack to the high section.

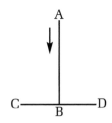

Movement 4a: Remain in stance and make a grasping motion with the left hand.

Meaning: grabbing the opponent's wrist.

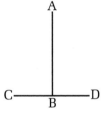

Movement 4b: Step forward with the left foot into a left forward stance facing B and execute a middle target punch with the right hand while pulling the left hand back to chamber.

Meaning: pulling the opponent close and stepping in to deliver a counterattack.

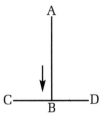

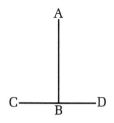

Movement 5: Remain in stance and execute a knife-hand block with the right hand.

Meaning: defense against an attack to the high section.

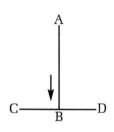

Movement 6a: Make a grasping motion with the right hand.

Meaning: Grab the opponent's wrist.

Movement 6b: Step forward with the right foot into a right forward stance facing B and execute a middle target punch with the left hand as the right hand draws back to chamber.

Meaning: pulling the opponent closer and stepping in to counterattack.

Movement 7: Remain in stance and execute a knife-hand block with the left hand.

Meaning: defense against an attack to the high section.

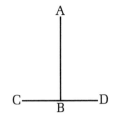

Movement 8a: Execute a side kick toward B with the left foot, Yell, *"Ki-Hop!"*

Meaning: counterattack.

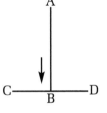

Movement 8b: Step down with the left foot into a forward stance facing B and execute a down block with the left arm.

Meaning: defense against an attack to the low section.

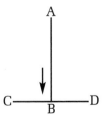

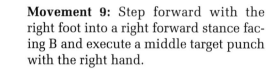

Movement 9: Step forward with the right foot into a right forward stance facing B and execute a middle target punch with the right hand.

Meaning: counterattack.

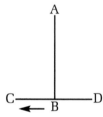

Movement 10: Turn 270° left into a left back stance facing C and execute an outer arm block with the left arm as the right arm guards the middle section.

Meaning: defense against an attack to the high section.

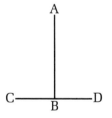

Movement 11a: Remain in stance and circle left arm to the outside.

Meaning: pushes opponent's attacking arm away.

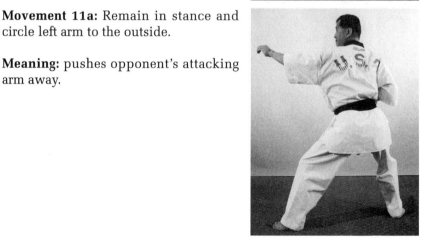

Movement 11b: Remain in stance and draw the left fist back to chamber as the right hand reaches toward C and makes a grabbing motion.

Meaning: grabbing the opponent's clothes.

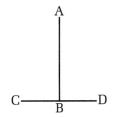

Movement 11c: Remain in stance and execute a middle target punch with the left hand as right hand draws back.

Meaning: pulls opponent close to counterattack.

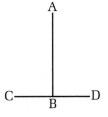

Movement 12a: While stepping forward with the right foot into a right back stance facing C, execute a rising block with the left arm as left hand makes a grasping motion.

Meaning: defense against an attack to the high section and immediately grabbing the opponent's wrist.

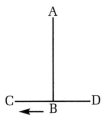

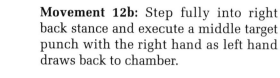

Movement 12b: Step fully into right back stance and execute a middle target punch with the right hand as left hand draws back to chamber.

Meaning: pulls opponent close to counterattack.

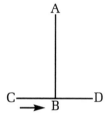

Movement 13: Turn 180° right into a right back stance facing D and execute an outer arm block with the right arm as the left arm guards the middle section.

Meaning: defense against an attack to the high section.

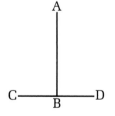

Movement 14a: Remain in stance and circle right arm to the outside.

Meaning: pushes opponent's attacking arm away.

Movement 14b: Remain in stance and draw the right fist back to chamber as the left hand reaches toward B and makes a grabbing motion.

Meaning: grabbing the opponent's clothes.

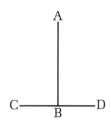

Movement 14c: Remain in stance and execute a middle target punch with the right hand as the left hand draws back.

Meaning: pulling the opponent close to counterattack.

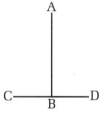

Movement 15a: While stepping forward with the left foot into a left back stance facing D, execute a rising block with the right arm as right hand makes a grasping motion.

Meaning: defense against an attack to the high section and immediately grabbing the opponent's wrist.

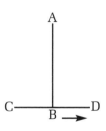

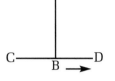

Movement 15b: Step fully into left back stance and execute a middle target punch with the left hand as right hand draws back to chamber.

Meaning: pulls opponent close to counterattack.

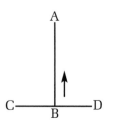

Movement 16: Turn 90° left into a left forward stance facing A and execute an outer arm block with the right arm.

Meaning: defense against an attack to the middle section.

Movement 17: Remain in stance and execute a middle target punch with the left hand.

Meaning: counterattack.

Movement 18a: Execute a front kick toward A with the right foot.

Meaning: second counterattack.

Movement 18b: Step down with the right foot into a right forward stance facing A and execute a middle target punch with the right hand.

Meaning: third counterattack.

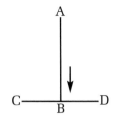

Movement 19: Slide right foot back into a right back stance facing A and execute a low double knife-hand block.

Meaning: defense against an attack to the low section.

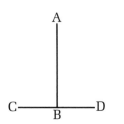

Movement 20a: Remain in stance and close right hand into a fist.

Movement 20b: Remain in stance and sweep the right arm up so that the fist slaps against the open palm of the left hand and then does an outer arm block.

Meaning: defense against attacks to the middle section and the high section.

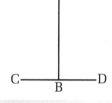

Movement 20c: Remain in stance and sweep the right arm down so that the right fist slaps against the open palm of the left hand and then does a down block.

Meaning: defense against attacks to the middle section and the low section.

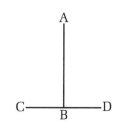

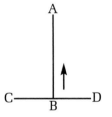

Movement 21: Turn toes of right foot inward into a horseback riding stance facing A and execute a simultaneous punch toward A with the right hand and a rising block with the left hand.

Meaning: defense against an attack to the high section and simultaneous counterattack against a different opponent.

Movement 22a: Shift weight forward to the right foot and spin around to the left.

Meaning: building momentum for a spinning kick.

Movement 22b: Continue to spin and hop onto left foot. Execute an inner crossing kick with the right foot to the open palm of the left hand.

Meaning: counterattack.

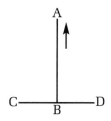

Movement 22c: Step down with the right foot into a right back stance facing A and execute a simultaneous punch toward A with the right hand and a rising block with the left hand.

Meaning: defense against an attack to the high section and simultaneous counterattack against a different opponent.

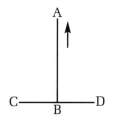

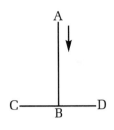

Movement 23: Turn torso and look 180° left as feet shift into a left back stance facing B and execute a partial mountain block using knife-hands.

Meaning: simultaneous defense against attacks to the high and low sections from opposite directions.

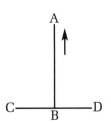

Movement 24: Turn torso and look 180° right as feet shift into a right back stance facing A and execute a partial mountain block using knife-hands.

Meaning: simultaneous defense against attacks to the high and low sections from opposite directions.

Movement 25a: Pivot 180° right on right foot into an upright stance facing B as hands slowly circle up and around.

Meaning: generating flowing energy with arms and hands.

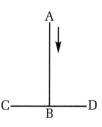

Movement 25b: Step forward with the right foot into a right tiger stance facing B as hands circle together and push strongly away from body with open hands as illustrated.

Meaning: pushing opponent's body away.

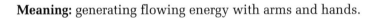

A
↑

C————————D
  B

Movement 26a: Slide right foot back into an upright stance facing B as hands slowly circle up and around.

Meaning: generating flowing energy with arms and hands.

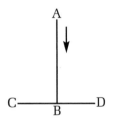

A
↓

C————————D
  B

Movement 26b: Step forward with the left foot into a left tiger stance facing B as hands circle together and push strongly away from body with open hands as illustrated.

Meaning: pushing opponent's body away.

Ready.

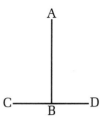

HAN SOO (WATER)

The primary characteristic of water is that it is readily adaptable to any situation. It adjusts its shape to conform to whatever environment it is presented with, and by doing so its basic nature remains unchanged and it is unharmed. The techniques of this form should be performed in a way that reflects the fluid adaptability of water.

Ready: Stand in an upright stance with feet together. Hands are held in knife-hand position low in front of the body with the left hand over the right.

Meaning: concentrating energy into the hands and arms.

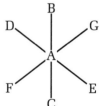

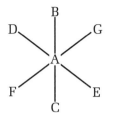

Movement 1: Step forward with the right foot into a right forward stance facing C and quickly execute simultaneous outer arm blocks. Hands are held in knife-hands with palms up.

Meaning: knocking opponent's hands lose from their grip on the front of the clothes.

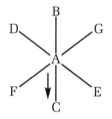

Movement 2: Step forward with the right foot into a right forward stance facing C and execute simultaneous inner hammer-fist strikes to the ribs.

Meaning: counterattack.

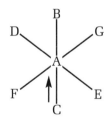

Movement 3: Step back toward B with right foot into a forward stance while the head looks back over left shoulder toward C. Execute a partial mountain block.

Meaning: defense against simultaneous attacks to the high and low sections from opposite directions.

Movement 4: Twist body around 180° left as left foot slides over into a left forward stance facing C and execute a middle target punch toward C with the right hand.

Meaning: counterattack.

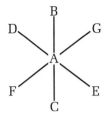

Movement 5: Step 180° left toward B with the left foot while the head looks back over the right shoulder toward C. Execute a partial mountain block.

Meaning: defense against simultaneous attacks to the upper and lower sections from opposite directions.

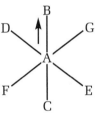

Movement 6: Twist body around 180° right as right foot slides over into a right forward stance facing C and execute a middle target punch toward C with the left hand.

Meaning: counterattack.

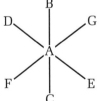

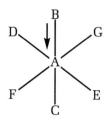

Movement 7: Step back toward A with the right foot toward into a right forward stance while head looks back over the left shoulder toward C. Execute a partial mountain block.

Meaning: defense against simultaneous attacks to the upper and lower sections from opposite directions.

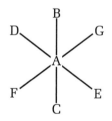

Movement 8: Twist body 180° left as the left foot slides over into a left forward stance facing C and execute a middle target punch toward C with the right hand.

Meaning: counterattack.

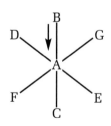

Movement 9: Step forward with the right foot into a right forward stance facing C and execute simultaneous outer arm blocks. Hands are held in knife-hands with the palms up.

Meaning: knocking opponent's hands loose from their grip on the front of the clothes.

Movement 10: Step 60° left with the left foot into a left forward stance facing E. Execute a simultaneous palm block with the right hand and an arcing-hand attack to the throat with the left hand.

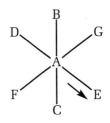

Meaning: defense against an attack to the middle section and simultaneous counterattack.

Movement 11: Step forward with the right foot into a reverse tiger stance facing E and execute simultaneous uppercut knuckle-fist strikes to the middle section.

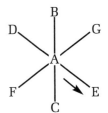

Meaning: second counterattack.

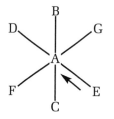

Movement 12: Step back toward A with left foot into a horseback riding stance with head facing forward. Strike open palm of left hand with right fist.

Meaning: Catch opponent's head with left palm as he or she collapses from the previous counterattack and deliver a finishing counterattack to the side of head.

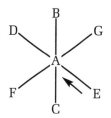

Movement 13: Pivot on left foot, moving right foot back toward A into a left back stance facing E and execute a low knife-hand block with the left arm and a simultaneous knife-hand rising block with the right arm.

Meaning: defense against simultaneous attacks to the upper and lower sections from different directions.

Movement 14: Shift weight back to right foot and raise left foot as both fists are pulled to the right hip.

Meaning: concentrating energy in preparation to kick.

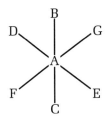

Movement 15a: Execute a side kick toward G with the left foot.

Meaning: counterattack.

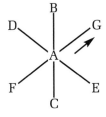

Movement 15b: Step down toward G with the left foot into a left forward stance facing G and execute a knife-hand rising block with the left arm and a simultaneous knife-hand strike to the neck with the right hand.

Meaning: defense against an attack to the upper section and simultaneous counterattack.

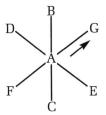

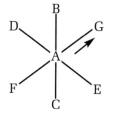

Movement 16a: Execute a front kick toward G with the right foot.

Meaning: second counterattack.

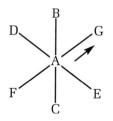

Movement 16b: Step down with right foot toward G and bring left foot forward into a twist stance facing G and execute a high target back-fist strike toward G with the right hand. Yell, "*Ki-hop!*"

Meaning: finishing counterattack.

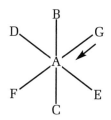

Movement 17: Step out with left foot into a horseback riding stance facing A and execute a knife-hand attack to the neck toward A with the left hand.

Meaning: preemptive counterattack.

Movement 18a: Execute an inner crossing kick to palm of extended left arm with the right foot.

Meaning: Hold opponent by the back of the head to deliver a counterattack.

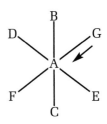

Movement 18b: Step down with the right foot toward A into a horseback riding stance facing A and deliver an elbow strike to the left palm with the right elbow.

Meaning: Continue holding opponent's head and deliver a finishing counterattack.

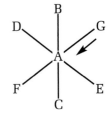

Movement 19a: Slide the left foot to the right foot while keeping knees bent and bring both fists to the left hip.

Meaning: concentrating energy into the arms and legs in preparation for action.

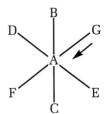

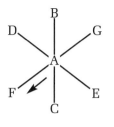

Movement 19b: Step out toward F with the right foot into a forward stance facing F and execute a palm block with the left hand and a simultaneous arcing-hand counterattack to the throat.

Meaning: defense against an attack to the middle section and simultaneous counterattack.

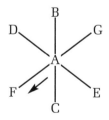

Movement 20: Step forward toward F with the left foot into a reverse tiger stance facing F and execute simultaneous knuckle-fist uppercut strikes to the middle section.

Meaning: second counterattack.

Movement 21: Step back toward A with the right foot into a horseback riding stance facing A and strike the palm of the right hand with the left fist.

Meaning: Catch opponent's head with right palm as he or she collapses from the previous counterattack and deliver a finishing counterattack to the side of head.

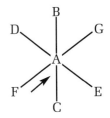

Movement 22: Step back toward A with the left foot into a back stance facing F and execute a simultaneous knife-hand down block with the right arm and a knife-hand rising block with the left arm.

Meaning: defense against simultaneous attacks to the low section and high section from different directions.

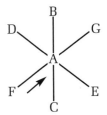

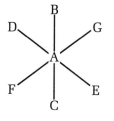

Movement 23: Shift weight back to left foot and pick up right foot.

Meaning: concentrating energy in preparation to kick.

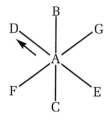

Movement 24a: Execute a side kick toward D with the right foot.

Meaning: counterattack.

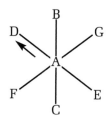

Movement 24b: Step down toward D with the right foot into a right forward stance facing D and execute a simultaneous knife-hand rising block with the right arm and a knife-hand strike to the neck with the left hand.

Meaning: defense against an attack to the high section and simultaneous counterattack.

Movement 25a: Execute a front kick toward D with the left foot.

Meaning: second counterattack.

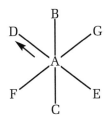

Movement 25b: Step down toward D with the left foot and draw the right foot forward into a twist stance facing D and execute a high target back-fist strike toward D with the left hand. Yell, "*Ki-hop!*"

Meaning: finishing counterattack.

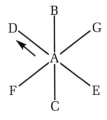

Movement 26: Step toward A with the right foot into a horseback riding stance facing A and execute a knife-hand strike to the neck with the right hand.

Meaning: preemptive counterattack.

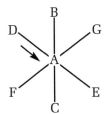

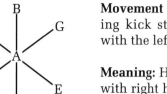

Movement 27a: Execute an inner crossing kick strike to palm of right hand with the left foot.

Meaning: Hold back of opponent's head with right hand to deliver second counterattack.

Movement 27b: Step down with the left foot into a horseback riding stance facing A and execute an elbow strike to the right palm with the left elbow.

Meaning: finishing counterattack.

Ready.

ILL YO (ONENESS)

The ultimate objective of Buddhism is to achieve a state of one-ness where mind, body and spirit are unified. Thought, action and will become one and the same thing. This integration of the three human aspects is the ultimate goal of Tae Kwon Do. The techniques of this form should be done with complete focus of concentration so that no thoughts or distractions disturb the flow of the form.

Ready: Stand in an upright position with the feet together. Slowly bring hands up to chin level so that the left hand wraps around the right fist.

Meaning: concentrating energy into the hands, but concealing it behind the open left hand.

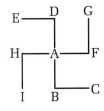

Movement 1: Step forward with the left foot toward B into a left back stance facing B and execute a double knife-hand block.

Meaning: defense against an attack to the high section.

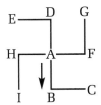

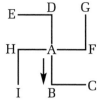

Movement 2: Step forward with the right foot toward B into a right forward stance facing B and execute a middle target punch toward B with the right hand.

Meaning: counterattack.

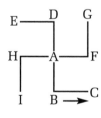

Movement 3: Step 90° left toward C with the left foot into a left back stance facing C and execute a simultaneous down block with the left hand and rising block with the right hand.

Meaning: defense against simultaneous attacks to the high and low sections from different directions.

Movement 4: Step 90° left toward A with the left foot into a left back stance facing A and execute a double knife-hand block.

Meaning: defense against an attack to the high section.

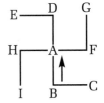

Movement 5: Remain in stance and execute a middle section punch toward A with the right hand.

Meaning: counterattack.

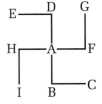

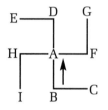

Movement 6: Step forward toward A with the right foot and quickly bring the left foot up behind the right knee. Execute a palm block with the left hand and a middle target spear-fingers strike toward A with the right hand. Yell, "*Ki-hop!*"

Meaning: defense against an attack to the middle section and simultaneous finishing counterattack.

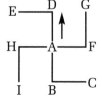

Movement 7: Execute a side kick toward D with the left foot.

Meaning: Preemptive counterattack.

Movement 8: Step down toward D with the left foot into a left back stance facing D and execute a high X block.

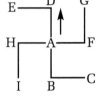

Meaning: defense against an attack to the upper section.

Movement 9a: Open hands and rotate them in a counterclockwise motion until both palms face upward.

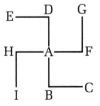

Meaning: Left hand sweeps opponent's arm aside as right hand pulls free.

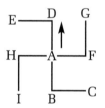

Movement 9b: Step forward toward D with the right foot into a right forward stance facing D and execute a middle target punch toward D with the right hand.

Meaning: counterattack.

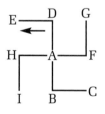

Movement 10: Step 90° left toward E with the left foot into a left back stance facing E and execute a simultaneous down block with the left arm and a rising block with the right arm.

Meaning: defense against simultaneous attacks to the low and high sections from different directions.

Movement 11: Step 90° left toward A with the left foot into a left back stance facing A and execute a double knife-hand block.

Meaning: defense against an attack to the upper section.

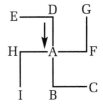

Movement 12: Remain in stance and execute a middle target punch toward A with the right hand.

Meaning: counterattack.

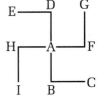

Movement 13: Step forward toward A with the right foot and quickly bring the left foot up behind the right knee. Execute a palm block with the left hand and a middle target spear-fingers strike toward A with the right hand. Yell, *"Ki-hop!"*

Meaning: defense against an attack to the middle section and simultaneous finishing counterattack.

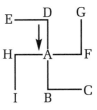

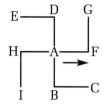

Movement 14: Execute a side kick toward F with the left foot.

Meaning: preemptive counterattack.

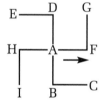

Movement 15: Step down toward F with the left foot into a left forward stance facing F and execute a high X block.

Meaning: defense against an attack to the high section.

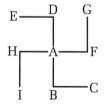

Movement 16a: Open hands and rotate them in a counterclockwise motion until both palms face upward.

Meaning: Left hand sweeps opponent's arm aside as right hand pulls free.

Movement 16b: Step forward with the right foot toward F into a right forward stance facing F and execute a middle target punch toward F with the right hand.

Meaning: counterattack.

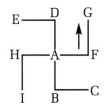

Movement 17: Step 90° left toward G with the left foot into a left back stance facing F and execute a simultaneous down block with the left hand and rising block with the right hand.

Meaning: defense against simultaneous attacks to the upper and lower sections from different directions.

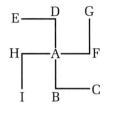

Movement 18: Slowly pivot 90° left on right foot into an upright stance facing A and draw both fists back to chamber.

Meaning: concentrating energy in the body in preparation for action.

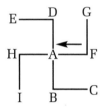

Movement 19a: Execute a front kick toward A with the right foot.

Meaning: preemptive counterattack.

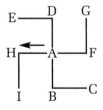

Movement 19b: Execute a flying side kick toward H with the left foot.

Meaning: finishing counterattack.

Movement 19c: Land in a left back stance facing H and execute a high X block.

Meaning: defense against an attack to the high section.

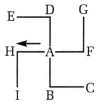

Movement 20a: Open hands and rotate them in a counterclockwise motion until both palms face upward.

Meaning: Left hand sweeps opponent's arm aside as right hand pulls free.

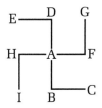

Movement 20b: Step forward toward H with the right foot into a right forward stance facing H and execute a middle target punch toward H with the right hand.

Meaning: counterattack.

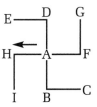

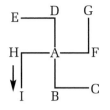

Movement 21: Step 90° left toward I with the left foot into a left back stance facing I and execute a simultaneous down block with the left arm and rising block with the right arm.

Meaning: defense against simultaneous attacks to the upper and lower sections from different directions.

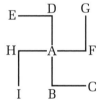

Movement 22: Slowly pivot 90° left on the right foot into an upright stance facing A and draw both fists back to chamber.

Meaning: concentrating energy in the body in preparation for action.

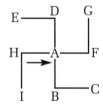

Movement 23a: Execute a front kick toward A with the left foot.

Meaning: preemptive counterattack.

Movement 23b: Execute a flying side kick toward F with the right foot.

Meaning: finishing counterattack.

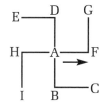

Movement 23c: Land in a right back stance facing F and execute a high X block.

Meaning: defense against an attack to the upper section.

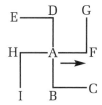

Ready.

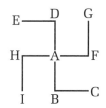

5 Sparring Techniques

One of the most fascinating and exciting aspects of Tae Kwon Do is sparring. It is through sparring that we can see how effective our fighting abilities are. The problem with sparring, however, is to balance realism with safety. Traditionally, the choices have either been to have some form of modified sparring with little or no protective gear, or to put on layers of thick padding to allow unrestricted use of techniques. Unfortunately, both of these approaches have drawbacks. Without any form of protection students can be seriously injured. Too much padding on the other hand can greatly inhibit movement. In either case, the realism of the situation is seriously compromised. In order to develop proper fighting reflexes, you must learn to counter and evade an opponent's blows while moving effectively to land your own. While bundling yourself in layers of padding will prevent injury, it can also very easily lead to the development of a careless attitude in which you unconsciously come to rely on the padding to protect you and don't develop the proper reflexes. Further, padding that is thick enough to completely protect the wearer from full power blows is also bulky and will slow you down. On the other hand, sparring without protection will definitely provide students with the incentive to block and evade. Knowing that a kick that can snap bone is being launched in your direction is a great motivator. But to allow the unrestricted use of such dangerous techniques can lead to serious injuries that will sideline practitioners before they have the chance to develop the fighting reflexes they need to prevent such injuries.

To address this issue of providing protection without inhibiting freedom of movement, Tae Kwon Do has evolved to include the use of specially designed, lightweight padding that protects the head, chest, forearms, shins and insteps (instep pads are optional in international competitions). While protecting the wearer from serious injury, it allows enough force to be felt by the wearer to lend a realistic feel to the sparring. Taking a kick to the body while wearing a WTF chest protector can jar a competitor, but will not result in broken ribs. A solid blow to the chest may knock the wind out of a competitor and a well-placed kick to the head* can even result in a knockout, but serious injuries are rare in modern Tae Kwon Do competitions. Because of the full head cover provided by the headgear, the bruises, black eyes and cauliflower ears that are common to boxers are not an issue either.

Along with providing a high degree of protection, the padding is also light enough to allow virtually unrestricted movement. Unencumbered by heavy, inflexible padding, competitors are free to utilize the full range of dynamic kicking techniques, which are the hallmark of Tae Kwon Do. It is precisely this dual aspect of Tae Kwon Do competitions that has allowed the art to grow into the immensely popular worldwide sport it has become. Spectators can thrill to witnessing matches in which competitors utilize a dazzling variety of quickly snapped, high, jumping and spinning kicks in a safe, sporting environment.

In this chapter we have compiled twenty sparring techniques that we have found to be especially effective in the ring. These techniques are presented as a follow-up to the techniques we included in our companion book for color belt level students. While the techniques in this book require a higher degree of skill to execute than those others, the techniques in the first book are by no means restricted to lower-ranking practitioners. They are solid, practical techniques that black belts and beginning students alike can use effectively in a sparring match. In this book, however, we will focus on techniques that require the advanced abilities black belt level practitioners have developed.

* Full power kicking techniques are only allowed in the adult divisions. In the junior divisions kicking to the head is only permitted if it is done with light contact so that no injury results.

Aside from mere physical abilities such as enhanced speed, power and flexibility, black belts should also have developed the ability to read an opponent. This is the single most important skill you need to sharpen if you want to be a successful competitor. By being able to read your opponents you will know what techniques they are going to throw before they do them. You will also be able to use this understanding to send misleading messages to your opponents about your own intentions, causing them to react in ways that will open them up for your own attack.

Learning to read an opponent comes from understanding certain basic principles about the nature of human movement. Put simply, movement is a process of throwing yourself off balance and catching yourself again before you fall. This idea can be illustrated by considering the simple process of walking. When you take a step, you lean your body forward and push off with one foot, in effect causing yourself to begin to fall. The nonpushing foot then steps forward and catches you. By continuing to push with the rear foot, you transfer your weight over the lead foot until you have taken a step. Running is an extension of this principle and jumping is a further extension of it. In fact, any movement of your body from one place to another is accomplished by this same general principle of off-balancing your weight and then quickly moving to catch yourself before you fall.

Once you understand the nature of human movement, you know what to look for in an opponent. In order to launch a rear leg kick, for example, your opponent *must* shift the weight to the front leg. To deliver a reverse punch the individual *must* drive with the rear leg and twist the hips and shoulders. These things cannot be helped. It would be physically impossible to do these techniques without shifting the body's weight in this manner. By observing the way your opponent moves when you are sparring, you will come to recognize specific shifts of the body that indicate what he or she is going to do.

A good way to learn about the way your opponent will move is to watch beginning Tae Kwon Do students as they spar. Beginning students feel awkward as they practice movements that are unfamiliar to them. As a result they tend to exaggerate their movements, making it very easy to see the way they shift their weight to deliver different kinds of techniques. Learn to recognize the way a person shifts weight to deliver each type of technique. The way a beginning student moves to launch a roundhouse kick is the same way that an advanced student must prepare for the same kick. Once you can read the intentions of beginning students, move on to intermediate-level students. You will notice that as people move up in rank they gradually refine their techniques so that their motions are not so obvious—they no longer telegraph their intentions as much. Yet you will still find that the same basic motions are there, however subtle. It is *impossible* to do away with the necessity to shift weight in order to deliver a technique. Even Tae Kwon Do masters must obey the laws of physics.

When you are sparring, an effective way to be aware of what your opponent is going to do is to watch the center of the chest. Some instructors recommend watching an opponent's eyes to see the person's intentions. This is because most people instinctively look where they are going to strike. While there is a lot that you can see by watching the eyes, it is the way the body moves that will tell you exactly what the opponent is going to do. Tae Kwon Do involves extensive use of foot techniques. By lowering your eyes slightly to center your vision on the body, you will be able to see all of your opponent in your peripheral vision. You will see the foot the moment it leaves the floor. And from the way he or she twists the hips, leans the shoulders and shifts weight, you will know exactly what your opponent is going to do with it.

Finally, keep in mind that your opponent is at the most vulnerable when moving. Whether taking a step or launching a technique, that the individual is moving means that he or she is off balance, if only for an instant. Remember that in order to move your opponent has become unbalanced and has committed to action. When you learn to read the body movements, and can predict what the individual is going to do, you can plan how to exploit that momentary instant of vulnerability.

Open vs. Closed Stances

There are always two things to keep in mind whenever you adopt a stance against an opponent—protection and the opportunity to attack. More than just assuming a good fighting stance with your hands in the correct guard position, you must also consider which lead you will use. Lead refers to the side of your body that is turned toward your opponent. Since most people are right-handed, a fighting stance with a left lead is the most common. Attacks with the lead side of the body tend not to be as powerful as attacks from the rear side. This is because rear side attacks travel a farther distance, thereby allowing you to build up more speed and power in your strike. Right-handed people therefore tend to want to keep their stronger, right side back. In this way they are able to quickly jab with their left side to stun or distract an opponent, while keeping their stronger right side back for finishing techniques.

The terms closed and open stances do not refer to a specific stance per se. Rather, they refer to the way you are standing relative to the way your opponent is standing. Photograph (A) illustrates a

a b

closed stance. This means that both competitors have assumed stances with the same lead and their chests facing in opposite directions. With their bodies turned in this way, it is difficult for either person to launch an effective attack with the rear foot (or hand). They are closed against an attack, hence the name *closed stance.* Not only would the opponent have more time to react to an attack launched from the rear, but the very way the body is turned naturally provides protection from attacks.

Photograph (B) shows an open stance. In this case, both competitors have taken stances with different leads, meaning that their chests are facing the same way. Even though they both have their arms up in proper guard position, notice how open each one is to a rear attack—hence the name *open stance.*

ATTACK TECHNIQUES

The ten examples we have included here are techniques that will enable you to score by taking the initiative. Since these techniques are launched against an opponent with the guard up, you must use a combination of surprise, speed and misdirection in order to open up your opponent and score. In taking the initiative you must either exploit an opening left by your opponent (which a black belt does not often do) or you must manipulate the person into creating an opening for you. You force your opponent to create an opening by moving or shifting your weight in such a way that you make the individual think you are going to do one thing while you set up for something else. Study the following examples to see some effective ways that this can be done. In each of these examples, the attacker will appear on the right.

Technique #1

Beginning in a closed stance (A), the attacker quickly jumps and changes the lead leg to achieve an open stance with the opponent (B). This makes the opponent vulnerable to a rear leg attack. Before the opponent can react and either change to a closed stance or launch an attack of his own, the attacker immediately fires off a running roundhouse kick to the body (C, D). Because you must assume that the

opponent will recognize his vulnerability and begin moving away to achieve cover when you change to an open stance, the running roundhouse is used to quickly close the distance while catching the individual in mid-motion. This technique requires speed and commitment by the attacker. If there is the least hesitation between the change in cover and the kick, the opponent will have time to react and the attack will not score.

Technique #2

From a closed stance (A) the attacker quickly jumps and. changes stance (B), once again opening up the opponent for a rear leg attack. The attacker then launches a rear leg roundhouse kick to the body (C) followed immediately by a spinning back kick (D, E). Here again you must anticipate that the opponent will recognize the vulnerability in an open stance and move to achieve protection. Because of this, the

first attack (the roundhouse) may not score. The immediate follow-up with the spinning back kick, however, will often catch your opponent off guard. Notice that by stepping down after delivering the initial roundhouse and spinning on your lead foot you will close the distance with your opponent as well as set yourself up for a powerful rear leg attack.

Technique #3
From a closed stance (A), the attacker launches a sliding side kick to the opponent's ribs (B, C). While a quickly executed lead leg kick may score, it is not as powerful as a rear leg attack. It is also likely that the

opponent will begin moving away from you as soon as you pick up your foot. If the opponent is moving away from you when the kick lands, it is probable that the kick will not have enough power to score. Having lulled the opponent into believing that the attack is over, the attacker immediately steps down and launches a jumping spinning roundhouse kick to the middle (D, E, F). This surprising change in direction allows you to land what is in effect a rear leg kick to the opponent's unprotected middle. Although the kick is actually begun from a closed stance, by jumping and spinning the kick is delivered as if it were launched from an open stance (D). The jumping-spinning action also allows you to quickly close the distance between yourself and the opponent before he or she can react.

Technique #4

From an open stance (A), the attacker picks up the lead foot and slides in (B), faking a lead leg attack. Once having closed the distance, the attacker immediately steps down and launches a rear leg roundhouse kick to the middle (C, D) as the opponent moves to change cover. Since they began in open stances, the opponent is aware of vulnerability when the attacker moves to close the distance between them. The attacker has planned for this, however, and follows up the first attack with an immediate second roundhouse kick with the other leg (E, F). Notice that since

the opponent has changed cover, he has actually positioned himself in an open stance for the attacker's second kick—which scores.

Technique #5

Starting in a closed stance (A), the attacker opens with a pushing kick using the rear leg (B) as the opponent attempts to step back out of range. Although a pushing kick will not score a point, it allows the attacker to push the opponent's body around to the opposite lead (C). With the opponent in position and before consolidating the stance, the attacker scores with a running roundhouse kick (C, D). Not only does the running kick pack a bigger punch, it is necessary to close the distance to the opponent, who has moved away.

Technique #6

From a closed stance (A), the attacker launches a rear leg round-house kick to the ribs (B). In order for a roundhouse to the ribs to score, the kick must be slipped in under the opponent's leading elbow. This is very difficult to do since by simply bringing the elbow down the opponent can protect the ribs. Because it is unlikely that a single, direct technique will score, the attacker immediately fires off a second roundhouse kick with the other foot (C). Momentarily over-whelmed by the suddenness of this dual attack, the opponent is

unprepared for the jumping roundhouse kick to the head that the at-tacker launches without returning the foot to the floor (D, E). When done properly, this technique can result in a knockout. To be effec-tive however, the kicks must be fired off very quickly and without hesitation.

Technique #7

Starting from an open stance (A), the attacker jumps to switch to a closed stance (B). By switching from an open stance to a closed stance the at-tacker gives the impression that the tactics will be defensive rather than offensive. Having lulled the opponent into a feeling of security, the at-tacker then leaps in and launches a jumping hook kick to the head (C, D, E). Although lead side attacks are generally not as powerful as rear side attacks, the combination of the leaping motion with the quick snap of the heel in the hook kick makes this an effective technique.

Technique #8

From a closed stance (A), the attacker begins by spinning around to fake a spinning back kick (B, C). The purpose of this is twofold. First, by using a spinning step the attacker closes the distance to the opponent. Second, this encourages the opponent to expect that the attacker will continue to use the spinning momentum built up and follow up with something like a rear leg roundhouse. In this case however, the attacker jumps (D) and delivers a spinning back kick in the other direction (E), catching the opponent off guard. Effective attacking techniques often require you to

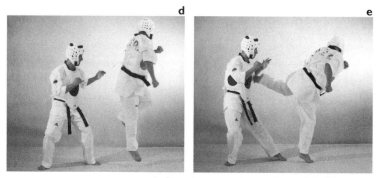

misdirect an opponent into thinking you are going to do one thing when in fact you are setting the individual up for something else.

Technique #9

From an open stance (A), the attacker brings the rear leg forward (B), giving the opponent the impression that you are launching a direct, rear leg attack to take advantage of the open stance. Although the opponent starts to move away as soon as the attacker begins to move, the attacker's forward movement has closed the distance between them. Without setting the foot down, the attacker springs up (C) and spins (D) to launch a jumping, spinning hook kick to the opponent's head (E, F).

A solid blow from this technique can result in a knockout. Here again, speed and misdirection are the key. While the opponent is reacting to what appears to be a simple rear leg attack, you use the momentum of the initial motion to catapult yourself into a powerful technique that overwhelms the opponent. Like any attacking technique, you must not hesitate once you start to move or you will give your opponent the chance to react.

Technique #10

From a closed stance (A) the attacker lunges forward (B) and launches an immediate rear leg axe kick to the head (C, D). This is a popular tournament technique because there is no way to block the kick. An axe kick drives straight down on the opponent's head, using gravity and the attacker's body mass to add speed and power to the blow. If the opponent does not move out of the way as soon as the attacker begins to move, there is nothing he or she can do to avoid being hit.

COUNTERATTACK TECHNIQUES

Although it may seem to contradict common sense, it is often easier to score against an opponent who is launching an attack than by initiating an attack of your own. This is because while attacking the individual is essentially off balance. With the leg extended the weight is shifted away from the body's normal center of gravity, making one

unstable. Additionally, the person is no longer shielded in a proper
fighting stance. When you can accurately read an opponent's body language and can predict the technique the person is going to throw, you
will know how the opponent is going to be exposed. Your properly
timed counterattack can then catch the individual at the moment of vulnerability. To take advantage of such an opening, which lasts only a
moment, you must perfect your timing and fully commit yourself to
your own technique. If you hesitate, you are lost. The following examples illustrate effective counters to techniques you will face in a
sparring situation. Just as with the examples of attack techniques, in
each example here the person counterattacking will appear on the right.

Technique #1

From a closed stance (A), the attacker skips forward (B) to throw a lead
leg roundhouse kick to the middle. By watching the way the attacker
moves, the defender recognizes the attack and responds by stepping *toward* the attacker and blocking while throwing a simultaneous jab to
the solar plexus (C). Since it is difficult to generate sufficient power to
score a point by punching with the lead hand, the defender finishes by
following up with an immediate rear leg roundhouse kick to the middle (D, E) while the opponent is still bringing a leg back down to regain
balance. Notice that when the defender stepped forward to block the

attacker's roundhouse (C), the defender moved into an open stance, allowing the rear leg be brought into play. This technique works because the roundhouse kick is one of the few kicks it is possible to evade by stepping toward the opponent. Unlike kicks such as the front kick or side kick, which move in a straight line toward the target, the roundhouse kick circles around to strike at a 90° angle. If you time your response properly, you can move inside the arc of a roundhouse and bring yourself out of the effective range of the kick. You must remain alert to what your opponent is doing however, and move immediately.

Technique #2

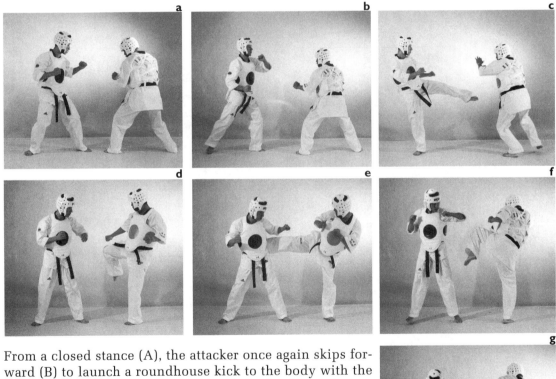

From a closed stance (A), the attacker once again skips forward (B) to launch a roundhouse kick to the body with the lead leg (C). This time, the defender slides *back* out of range (C). As the attacker lowers the foot, the defender launches a rear leg roundhouse to the ribs (D, E) followed immediately by a second rear leg roundhouse to the middle (F, G). Here, the defender surprises the opponent with a quick double technique. Knowing that it is difficult to actually score with a rear leg strike from a closed stance, the defender uses the first kick to set up an open stance where the second kick can score.

Technique #3

From a closed stance (A), the attacker launches a rear leg axe kick (B). Recognizing the attack, the defender slides back out of range of the kick (B). As the attacker's foot moves harmlessly through the arc of its swing

(C), the defender launches a rear leg roundhouse kick to the middle (D) before the attacker can regain balance. Notice that as the attacker brings the foot down (C), he has taken an open stance. The defender takes advantage of this to launch a corresponding rear leg counterattack. Be aware that in order for this technique to work, you must recognize the attacker's technique as an axe kick and move out of the way *immediately*. Because of the speed of an axe kick, it will score against you if you do not step back as soon as the attacker moves.

Technique #4

From a closed stance (A), the defender steps forward with a change step (B). By doing so, he has not only closed the distance between them, but also changed the lead so that the defender is now standing in an open stance. Seeking to take advantage of this opportunity, the attacker launches a rear leg roundhouse kick to the middle (C). Here, the defender has purposefully lured the opponent into using a rear

leg attack. The defender counters by sidestepping to the back right to block the kick (D). Notice that by stepping back and to the side, the defender has remained positioned in an open stance. From here, the defender fires off a rear leg roundhouse to the middle to score (E).

Technique #5

From a closed stance (A), the attacker skips forward (B) to throw a lead leg axe kick (C). Recognizing the attack, the defender spins (D) to deliver a spinning hook kick to the middle (E) before the attacker's foot has even touched down. The spinning motion of the defender's

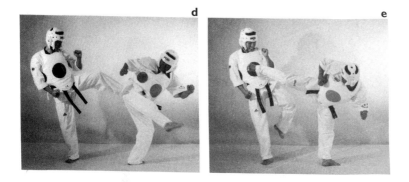

counterattack allows the head to move out of the line of the axe kick while remaining within range to land one's own kick. Because it comes straight down, the effective strike zone of an axe kick is in a very narrow area which can be avoided by moving slightly to one side or the other. It is also a technique that is impossible to stop once you commit to it. The defender uses his understanding of the limitations of the kick to launch a counterattack while the attacker still has the leg extended and is vulnerable.

Technique #6

Here, the attacker has crowded close to the defender (A). Although they are in a closed stance, the defender is wary of the attacker being so close and uses a pushing side kick to drive the attacker back (B). Pushed away, the attacker tries to take advantage of the fact that the defender's leg is extended. The attacker turns to spin (C), using the momentum of the defender's own pushing kick to throw a spinning hook kick to the defender's head (D). By remaining alert, the defender was aware that the attacker was readying a spinning kick and slid back out of range (D). As the kick passes, the defender launches a rear leg roundhouse kick to the middle (E), catching the attacker before the person is able to regain balance (F).

Technique #7

From an open stance (A), the attacker tries to score with a quick rear leg roundhouse to the middle (B). Aware of vulnerability to such an attack, the defender fires off a reverse punch to the middle the instant that the attacker beings to move (B). He follows this with an immediate rear leg roundhouse kick to the ribs (C), catching the attacker before the individual can regain balance. In this situation, the defender uses the position of being in an open stance to lure the opponent into striking. The exact type of kick the attacker uses is unimportant. The defender uses two pieces of information to turn the situation to advantage. First, you know that by throwing a rear leg kick the attacker must turn the chest directly toward you, momentarily exposing it. Second, you know that a hand technique can be launched faster than a foot technique, giving you a speed advantage. However, being close enough to land a punch means that you are also within range of the opponent. The follow-up kick not only ensures that you score but helps to keep the attacker at a distance. The key to this technique is speed. You must move the instant your opponent does or that individual's technique will land first.

Technique #8

From an open stance (A), the attacker slides in to close the distance between him/herself and the defender (B) and set up for a rear leg attack. The defender steps back using a change step. (C) With the opportunity

to land a rear leg attack gone, the attacker skips in to throw a lead leg roundhouse kick (D). The defender counters by spinning (E) to throw a jumping spinning back kick to the middle (F). Although it may appear that the defender is taking a risk by not blocking the attacker's kick, the action of jumping and spinning moves the individual out of the effective range of the roundhouse.

Technique #9

From a closed stance (A), both the attacker and the defender fire off simultaneous rear leg roundhouse kicks, which results in a clash (B). While the attacker simply lowers the kicking foot to the floor, the defender brings the foot *back* to the rear (C), and immediately spins in the opposite direction (D) to throw a spinning hook kick at the attacker's head (E, F). Here, the defender does not let such a clash become a distraction. Realizing that simply lowering the foot to the floor will leave one dangerously close to the opponent, the defender immediately spins in the opposite direction, catching the attacker off guard. Often competitors will allow themselves to get distracted when their techniques don't go as planned. In this example, the defender took advantage of this to reverse the movement and surprise the opponent.

Technique #10
From a closed stance (A), the attacker lunges in to attack (B). Without waiting to see what attack is coming, the defender immediately spins (C) and jumps (D) to launch a jumping spinning hook kick to the head (E). In this situation, the defender is making good use of the principle

that an opponent is most vulnerable while attacking to land one's own counterattack. By jumping and spinning the defender also moves out of line of the opponent's attack. For this technique to succeed you must react the instant your opponent moves.

6 Self-Defense Techniques

A self-defense situation is much different from a sparring competition. In a competition there are rules that restrict you (and your opponent) to specific valid targets and limit the types of techniques that can be used. None of that is true in a self-defense situation however. The very definition of self-defense is to protect yourself from harm. If you ever find yourself in a situation in which you are physically threatened, you must use whatever means necessary to protect yourself. Techniques such as sweeping (knocking an opponent's legs out from under him), grabbing and throwing, which are not allowed in a sparring match, represent an additional arsenal that should be exploited if you are ever forced to protect yourself. Further, when you are defending yourself, an opponent's entire body becomes open to attack, allowing you to target the most vulnerable areas to dispose of the person as quickly as possible.

As a black belt you have developed skills that can be very dangerous. For example, the amount of force necessary to break two 3/4-inch pine boards will also shatter human ribs. Blows with this type of power directed at the right areas on a person's body can cripple or even kill. Controlling this type of power is a great responsibility. Legally, the use of deadly force is only allowed when your own life (or another person's) is threatened. If your life is not in jeopardy but you believe that physical harm is imminent, a lesser amount of force must be used. Basically, you are allowed to use only as much force as necessary to stop the assailant from causing the harm he intends. Be aware that as a trained martial artist you can be held to a higher standard than an untrained person. In many places a black belt is automatically considered to be armed and any fighting situation you become involved in will be judged accordingly. But this is only from a legal standpoint. As a student of Tae Kwon Do, you also have a moral imperative *not* to misuse what you have learned. Our art is one of self-improvement and discipline. By the time you achieve the level of black belt you should be conscious of the serious injury you can inflict. *You* know you can seriously hurt someone, so there is no need to beat an attacker to a pulp if you can simply avoid the entire situation instead. Of course you must protect yourself if you are attacked, but you must also be confident enough in your abilities that you don't feel the need to prove anything. In such situations we advise the use of a very simple but effective tactic—run away.

Ironically, many martial artists find that they never have to use their skills. People who are truly confident in themselves and their abilities exude an aura that tends to ward off many would-be attackers. Muggers and other assailants rely on their instincts much more than most people do today. They depend on their instincts to select their victims and have developed the ability to read others. A mugger wants your money, not a fight. If he senses that you would not be an easy target, he is likely to move on to someone who will not pose a threat. This is not to say that as a black belt you should walk through dark alleys with $100 bills sticking out of your pockets. You must exercise discretion and take commonsense precautions. Remember also that *no one* is invulnerable. A lucky blow by an assailant or a surprise attack from behind can finish even the most accomplished martial artist.

In this chapter we have put together seven examples of practical self-defense techniques. You will notice that we have not limited the techniques to strict Tae Kwon Do moves. We have made free use of grabbing and joint manipulation techniques as well as sweeps and throws. While in the ring your honor as a Tae Kwon Do student requires you to adhere to the rules of competition; when you are faced with a defensive situation, your objective is to protect yourself. There is no such thing as a *fair* fight. A fight is a situation in which your physical safety is being threatened. You did not create the situation, and if you cannot avoid it, you must do everything in your power to end it as quickly as possible and walk away intact.

Technique #1

In this first sequence, the attacker grabs the front of the defender's clothes (A) either as an attempt to intimidate or in preparation to punch with his free hand. Instead of trying to pull himself free, the grandmaster reaches across to the little finger edge of the attacker's hand (B, C), grasping it firmly. Once he has grabbed the hand he twists while he uses his free hand to press against the attacker's elbow, locking his arm straight (D, E). Notice in (E) how the grandmaster flexes the attacker's wrist and bends himself at the waist to use his weight to put pressure on the elbow. Also note that the grandmaster has stepped in front of the attacker's lead foot, bringing their hips into alignment. This positioning allows the grandmaster to have the best control of the attacker with the least exertion. Next, slipping the fingers of his left hand around to the inside of the attacker's elbow, the grandmaster pulls around and down on it, causing the elbow to bend while he keeps the wrist flexed (F). It is very important to keep control of the opponent's arm in this way. It is this hold that gives the grandmaster control of the attacker's entire body. Note that the grandmaster has also stepped back

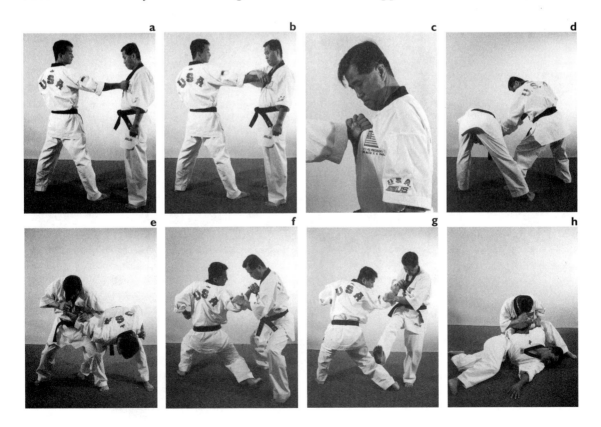

with his foot so that he is perpendicular to the opponent and lowered himself into a horseback riding stance. This movement allows him to use his body's weight to manipulate the attacker instead of trying to muscle him with his arms alone. With the attacker now off balance, the grandmaster raises his leg and sweeps the attacker's near leg (G), throwing him to the ground (H). Throughout this movement the grandmaster retains control of the attacker's arm and wrist, keeping him helpless. Since the attacker did not brandish a weapon or actually attempt to hit him, the grandmaster simply maintains the submission hold on him instead of finishing him with a strike.

Technique #2

Here, the attacker tries to control the grandmaster's hands by grabbing his sleeves from the rear (A). This type of attack is often used by one person to hold someone helpless so that another attacker can strike. Ignoring the hold, the grandmaster raises his arms to both sides (B) and steps back behind the attacker's foot as he ducks under his left arm. (Although we have shown this technique on the left, it can be done to either side.) As he slides his head under the attacker's arm, the grandmaster turns his left hand palm up and grabs the attacker's left forearm (C). At the same time he slides his right arm up the attacker's back until

his right forearm is resting on the triceps muscle of the attacker's left arm (the rear of the upper arm). The grandmaster then drops to his right knee (D), using his weight to lock the attacker's arm straight. The pain and pressure on his elbow forces the attacker to drop to the ground. Once the attacker is down, the grandmaster uses his left thigh to help keep the attacker's arm locked straight. Be aware that this technique will only work if the attacker keeps his grip on the defender's sleeves. If he releases you when you move to step under his arm, simply take another step back and you will have freed yourself from his hold.

Technique #3

In this scenario, the attacker attempts to land a right hook on the grand-master's jaw. After blocking the punch with a left knife-hand block to the wrist (B), the grandmaster continues to sweep his arm out and down so that he can grab the attacker's hand with both of his hands (C). Note the way the grandmaster holds the attacker's hand in (D). This is important because it allows him to control that hand, arm and ulti-mately the attacker's entire body. With the hand properly held, the

grandmaster continues to circle the attacker's arm in an upward arc as he steps under it (E). Once he has stepped under the arm, the master spins quickly to his right as he twists the attacker's captured hand and grasps it firmly with both hands (F). Take note of the way that the grandmaster has grabbed the attacker's *hand,* not his wrist, with both of his hands. This hold puts severe pressure on the wrist, causing ex-treme pain. From here he pulls the opponent's captured wrist in and down, bringing him to the floor (G). Once the attacker has been brought to the ground, additional pain can be caused by kneeling on the at-tacker's biceps muscle (the front of the upper arm).

Technique #4

Here, the attacker launches a high roundhouse kick with the left foot
(B). The grandmaster leans *toward* the attacker, bringing himself inside
the arc of the kick so that he can catch the force of the kick on his
shoulder (C). Notice that when the kick lands, the grandmaster raises
his hands so that his right hand is behind the attacker's leg while his
left is in front, effectively capturing the leg. The grandmaster then
slides his left foot behind the attacker's supporting ankle (D). By applying pressure with his left forearm to the attacker's thigh as he pivots
right, the grandmaster is able to throw the attacker to the ground,
where he finishes him with a punch to the solar plexus (E).

Technique #5

In this situation, the grandmaster is confronted by an attacker wielding
a knife (A). Anytime an attacker brandishes a weapon you must consider it an attack on your life. It then becomes imperative for you to
incapacitate him as quickly as possible. As the attacker lunges for a
stab to the abdomen (B), the grandmaster thrusts his hips back to move
his body out of range as he blocks the stabbing hand with a downward
X block. Notice that he does the block using knife-hands so he can grab.
Then, while keeping his left hand in position to prevent the attacker

from shoving the blade forward, the master reaches down with his right hand to grab the little finger edge of the attacker's hand and twists and flexes the wrist (C). Take note of how the grandmaster uses both hands to hold the attacker's hand. The proper grip is with thumbs pressed tightly into the back of the hand while the fingers grip the base of the thumb and the little finger edge of the hand. With the attacker held in this wrist lock, the grandmaster incapacitates him with a front kick to the solar plexus (D). As the attacker falls, the grandmaster maintains his hold on the wrist lock, keeping the arm extended and away from the attacker's body as he continues to twist the hand (E). This causes pain and weakness in the attacker's hand and wrist which makes him drop the knife.

Technique #6

Here, the grandmaster is confronted by two assailants. Attacker number one approaches from the front and threatens to punch, while attacker two approaches from the rear with a knife (A). As the first attacker throws a roundhouse punch to the face, the master counters with a knife-hand block to the wrist (B). Sweeping the attackers hand out and down, the grandmaster captures his hand and steps under it using the same movement demonstrated in technique #3 (C, D, E). In this scenario, the assailant with the knife is clearly the more dangerous

of the two. Although it may appear that the grandmaster has ignored this threat, that is not the case. Notice that by deflecting the first attacker's punch and securing him in a wrist lock, the grandmaster has moved out of range of the second attacker (E). As the second attacker now steps forward to strike with the knife (F), the grandmaster incapacitates him with a side kick to the ribs (G). With the second attacker out of the way (H), the grandmaster grabs the first attacker's hand tightly with both of his (I). From here, he steps back with his left leg and pivots to face in the opposite direction, pulling on the attacker's hand to throw him to the ground (J). Once the attacker has been thrown, further pain can be applied by kneeling on his arm.

Technique #7

Here, one attacker has grabbed the grandmaster from behind in a bear hug while a second attacker prepares to stab him from the front (A). First, the grandmaster dispatches the knife-wielding attacker with a quick front kick to the solar plexus as he moves in to strike (B). Having dispatched the first attacker, the grandmaster now drops low and raises the elbows to loosen the attackers hold as he grabs his arms (C). Note that he grabs the attacker's right elbow and steps forward slightly with his right foot. This is important because it sets up the next movements.

By bending forward at the waist and snapping his hips back quickly as he twists and brings his head to his left knee (D), the grandmaster is able to throw the attacker to the ground (E). The grandmaster now finishes the stunned attacker with a palm strike to the side of the jaw (F).

7 Breaking Techniques

Breaking techniques are the most dynamic way we have of demonstrating power. In Tae Kwon Do, power is generated through the use of focus—the ability to channel all of the strength and energy in your body to a specific point in space. In the same way that a magnifying glass can concentrate the sun's rays to a burning point, advanced practitioners can do the same with the power in their bodies, imbuing their strikes with incredible destructive force. Students below the level of black belt also perform breaking techniques. In fact, most schools require students to do a break for each promotion test. But the typical breaks done by color belt students are straightforward techniques against rigidly supported boards.* With the boards held securely in place, students are free to concentrate all of their attention on generating enough power to smash through them.

*   See the chapter on board breaking in our companion book *Tae Kwon Do,* for a description of proper board holding.

211

Black belt level techniques are different. Advanced breaking techniques are designed to show the level of precise control a person has developed over his or her focus. The ability to generate this concentration of energy against an unsupported target, against multiple targets, in different directions simultaneously, or while performing complex movements both on the ground and in the air demonstrate this control. While we cannot show every possible advanced breaking technique, we have included examples of breaks that illustrate different types of focus control. Once you have mastered a certain type of breaking technique, the level of difficulty can be increased by doing it as a speed break (see below), or by adding more boards or bricks.

Speed Break

Unlike simple breaking techniques in which the boards to be broken are strongly supported by one or more holders, a speed break relies on the speed and precision of the person performing the technique. Without the support of holders to keep the board in place, the person doing the break must strike with such speed that the hand (or foot) moves through the board so quickly that it breaks before it can fly away. The

person must also hit the board in precisely the right spot. This type of breaking requires a high degree of focus to accomplish. Here, Grandmaster Park demonstrates a speed punch break.

Multiple Station Break

Power and the ability to precisely deliver a technique are not the only hallmarks of advanced practitioners. When people can deliver such precisely controlled techniques one after the other, they can truly be said to have control of their focus. Multiple station breaks allow practitioners to demonstrate this advanced level of control. In a multiple station break, objects are broken one after the other in two or more locations using any combination of hand and/or foot techniques. Here,

Grandmaster Park demonstrates a two station break using a palm strike and a side kick.

Spinning Break

Black belts are expected to be able to deliver their techniques accurately. During a sparring competition or in a self-defense situation one must not only be able to deliver a quick and powerful technique but also be able to do so on target. Delivering devastating kicks while performing a complex movement such as spinning around demonstrates the precise control of advanced Tae Kwon Do practitioners. Here, Grandmaster Park demonstrates a spinning back kick break.

Jumping Break

Most breaking techniques are done while the person is in contact with the ground. This contact provides them with support for the technique, allowing them to throw their weight into the strike. In a jumping break, however, that support is gone. In order to perform such a break, the person must not only have a highly developed sense of focus, he or she must also have developed sufficient control of the body to perform complex movements in the air and touch down again in control. Here, Master Y. Kim demonstrates a jumping, spinning roundhouse kick.

Simultaneous Break

Simultaneous breaks are some of the most challenging because more than one object is broken at the same time. Unlike multiple station breaks, the person doing the break cannot focus one at a time on each object to be broken. Instead, the person must strike both objects simultaneously with sufficient force to break them. Often, this type of break involves a jumping technique in which the person must land under control after performing a complicated technique in midair. Here, Master Lee demonstrates a jumping double front kick.

Acrobatic Break

Many advanced practitioners develop their own signature breaking techniques. Often these techniques are developed for breaking (*kyuk pah*) competitions. In such a competition, judges look not only for power but for creativity and the level of difficulty involved. Since breaking competitors strive to create the most spectacular demonstrations possible, these types of breaks often involve acrobatics. The ability to perform a breaking technique as one is gyrating through the air shows exceptional agility and control of focus. Here, Master Jang demonstrates a back flip break using a front kick.

Concrete Break

Although many breaking techniques are done using wooden boards, advanced practitioners often perform breaking techniques on much harder things as well. Concrete, brick, ice and other materials are favorite breaking subjects because they require such a high degree of focus. Caution must be exercised when attempting such breaks, however, because these materials are stronger than human bone and injury can result if the technique is not done correctly. All of the energy in the breaker's body must be properly concentrated or the force of the strike can reflect back into the person's arm or leg. Here, Mister Gerrard demonstrates a palm break through concrete.

Speed Brick Break

At the beginning of this chapter we showed an example of a speed break against a board. This technique can also be done against much harder objects, such as bricks. These breaks demonstrate the highest degree of focus because the person not only has to strike hard enough to break something as tough as a brick, but must do so with sufficient speed to break it instead of simply knocking it over. This is the most difficult type of breaking technique.

This photograph was taken at a local charity event at which Grandmaster Park was called out of the audience to give an impromptu demonstration. Although unprepared, Grandmaster Park's precise control of focus enabled him to perform this impressive feat. Here, Grandmaster Park demonstrates a speed knifehand break through two unsupported bricks.

8 Opening Your Own School

TEACHING TAE KWON DO

Operating a Tae Kwon Do school is different from other types of commercial enterprises. As a business owner you must be concerned with the practical matters of keeping the business going. But if you focus only on the bottom line, you will never be a Tae Kwon Do instructor in the true sense. A true teacher of Tae Kwon Do is interested first and foremost in the growth and development of his or her students. Of course, if you do not pay attention to practical concerns, your school will not remain open for long and you will never have the chance to help your students to develop. It is the careful balance of these two components that marks a truly successful school.

Today, there are many commercially profitable martial arts schools filled with a dazzling variety of exotic training equipment and boasting a large student enrollment. Unfortunately, many such schools have become what are known in the business as "black belt factories." These are schools where students advance steadily through the ranks to achieve the level of black belt without developing the physical, mental

219

and spiritual characteristics of a true black belt. In the worst cases, students advance in rank simply by attending a certain number of lessons and then paying their promotion test fees. In effect, they are buying their belts. While students from such schools may have learned certain basic skills, their technique is usually not refined. More important, the mental discipline and self-control that should accompany development in Tae Kwon Do is absent. These schools are often operated by people who hold distorted views of the martial arts. To them, a school is simply a means to an end—a way to make a living. True teachers of Tae Kwon Do understand that the practice of any martial art is an end in itself, with promotion through the ranks simply being an indicator of the student's current level of development.

Misguided teachers often have been trained by teachers who themselves do not understand the true nature of their art. Such schools are dangerous because they spread a false idea of what the martial arts are. Most students from these schools eventually come to realize that what they have learned is hollow and without lasting value. Their techniques are inferior and ineffective due to improper training, and in many cases they come to view all martial arts as false. These students become disillusioned and turn their backs on the martial arts while thinking that the false impression they have is the truth. They never seek further instruction from a reputable school, thinking that there is nothing of value for them there. This is a loss both to the students and the martial arts community.

There is another type of school that is even more dangerous. In these schools, the development of fighting skills is paramount. Students drill and practice, often using brutal training methods, with a single purpose—to develop their bodies into lethal weapons. Omitted from their training, however, is any moral or philosophical basis underlaying their instruction. While to an outside observer these schools may appear to be the epitome of discipline, it is the discipline of intimidation. Raw, physical power is the only thing valued. Respect is shown only to those who have superior fighting abilities. If there is a philosophy underlying the training in these schools, it is to overcome your opponent **at any cost.** Yet, without a moral base, these martial artists are little more than thugs and bullies. No sane adult would hand a loaded gun to a child. In the same way, no responsible martial arts teacher should train students without making certain that the students have the proper moral grounding to know when it is appropriate to use the training they are receiving. The techniques of Tae Kwon Do, or any martial art, are *dangerous* and must be treated with the proper respect to prevent their misuse. True teachers understand that *they* are responsible for the way their students use their abilities, whether it is today, tomorrow or ten years from now.

Running a Reputable School

The first and foremost requirement you need to operate a reputable Tae Kwon Do school is the proper certification. Many people get a black belt and rush to open their own school. This is a mistake. Although a person may have earned a black belt from a WTF or USTU certified master, as a first degree black belt you are not yet fully qualified to op-

erate a school on your own. Starting at first degree, black belts are required to assist the master with running classes. This provides them with invaluable teaching experience under the watchful eye of a seasoned teacher. New black belts also have not yet fine-tuned their own techniques. While they may know how to perform the gross movements of a technique, they usually have not yet developed the fluid precision of someone who has truly mastered the art. Black belts below fourth degree are sometimes referred to as advanced students, students who have learned all of the basic techniques and are working to perfect them. Ironically, it is through teaching a technique, demonstrating it time and again and explaining how it is properly done and why, that a black belt comes to truly learn that technique.

For these reasons, it is very important that Tae Kwon Do students do not try to open a school before they are fully prepared. If owning your own school is a goal, you should talk to your master. He or she will be happy to share whatever information they have. Often, they will be willing to allow you greater responsibilities so that you can learn the details of how the school is run. Many masters also branch out and open satellite schools. Since the master cannot operate all of the schools alone, some students are needed to run those schools. Apprenticing in this way will allow you to learn a great deal about operating a school. It will take time, but in the long run you and your school will be better off if you learn the art and the business well.

Remember as well that when you put out a sign offering lessons in Tae Kwon Do you are representing yourself as a member of the Tae Kwon Do community. As such, you are honor bound to follow the regulations of our community. One of the most important rules we have is that schools can only be operated by fourth degree black belts and above (masters). As we mentioned, a *chokyonim* (first to third degree black belt) may manage a satellite school, but only under the direction of a certified master. The respect accorded to Tae Kwon Do instructors is something that can exist only as long as there is consistency in what people can expect when they walk into one of our schools.

Having seen the improper ways some schools are operated in the previous section, we will now examine the way a good Tae Kwon Do school is run. While there is no simple formula for what makes a competent teacher, there are certain basic traits that any teacher of quality possesses. More than anything else, a good teacher has the best interests of his or her students at heart. This is the single most important quality any teacher of substance must possess. The respect the students have for you will be based not so much on your physical abilities as on the relationship you establish with them. Respect is not something you can force someone to feel. Only when they know that you truly care about them will your students give you their trust and respect. Do not underestimate the importance of this. Students know when a teacher is being genuine and when a teacher is not. Any instructor who does not first respect his or her students will get students who have no respect for the instructor. Once this is gone, the students themselves will soon follow.

Not everyone teaches the same way. Each instructor brings his or her own unique personality to their teaching style. While there are as many different styles of teaching as there are instructors, all good teachers do follow the same basic principles. First, you must be comfortable with yourself and confident in your abilities. In part this comes from keeping yourself fit, both mentally and physically. There is no surer way to lose the respect of your students than not to practice what you preach. You must also keep yourself current with what is happening in the world of Tae Kwon Do so that you can speak with knowledge and authority. When you have confidence in yourself, this attitude is transmitted to your students. It is okay to make an occasional mistake or not have a ready answer all the time. No one is perfect. Remember that even as a teacher you are continuing to learn yourself. The study of Tae Kwon Do is *never* complete. If a situation arises that you don't have an answer for, don't be afraid to tell the student that you will have to think about it. You will look far better in the student's eyes if you take the time to come up with a well-thought-out response to a question or situation than if you are so concerned with always having the right answer at your fingertips that you give a wrong answer. This will destroy your credibility with your students faster than anything else and lose the one thing you need to be an effective teacher—their respect.

Remember that different students develop at different rates. Not everyone can grasp a new idea or technique immediately. Therefore, you must always be encouraging to your students, praising their accomplishments and helping them to overcome their mistakes without making them feel as if they have failed. You should *never* be negative. While you do have to correct their mistakes, you should do so in ways that are not demeaning. For example, instead of correcting a student by saying, "You did that wrong," comment on what was right and then suggest a better way to do the technique. *All* students can develop mastery of the techniques given enough time, patience and encouragement. Be especially aware that not everyone learns in the same way. If a student is having difficulty with a particular technique, rethink *your* teaching methods and try to connect with the student in a way that he or she understands better. Above all you must strive to build confidence in all of your students, particularly in the weaker ones. You should also try to pay attention to them as individuals. While individual attention is difficult to manage in large classes, try to find something to praise each student for. Even small gestures such as catching a student's eye and giving that individual a nod can have a great impact. This will let them know that you are aware of them personally and increase their sense of self-worth.

One of the most difficult things to keep in mind is that you should not promote students before they are ready or deserving. It is tempting (and easier) to promote students as a class, but it is not always the right thing to do. Just because students started their training together does not mean that they are automatically entitled to test for promotion at the same time. If a student has superior ability but only attends class infrequently, that student should be made to wait until he or she has attended more classes. Many teachers keep attendance cards, which are marked each time a student takes a class. This removes any ambiguity and gives you something objective to refer to if you ever do have to tell a student to wait until the next belt test. Allowing students to test without requiring them to put in a certain minimal level of effort encourages disrespect for the art. Remember, the practice of Tae Kwon Do is more than merely developing physical techniques. It involves respect for oneself and others as well as the art itself.

Other students may attend regularly, but may not have gained the same level of mastery that others at their level have. This is always a difficult situation because you do not want to discourage students. If students are truly not ready to advance to a higher level, however, promoting them when they have not sufficiently mastered the techniques at their level will only cheapen the belt they wear. Rank only has value when a student truly earns it. Remember also that students do not have to perfect every nuance of each technique before they advance. As long as a certain minimal level of competence is reached, and the student is trying his or her best, promotion is warranted. It is the perfection of character that is the ultimate aim of the art.

If a student is having difficulty, however, several options are available to a teacher. First, you can give that person more individual attention. Having the instructor take a personal interest in a student often encourages the student to strive harder and achieve more. Another effective approach is to involve the rest of the class. As the time for the next promotion test nears, encourage the more advanced students to work with those who are having difficulty. This strengthens the bonds among the students and encourages them to grow as a community.

Finally, at some time you may encounter students who behave in an inappropriate manner in spite of your best efforts to have them control themselves. They may bully or intimidate weaker students, treat the *dojang* with disrespect, or appear in a slovenly condition for class. Although it is extremely rare for a teacher to need to address inappropriate behavior more than once, students who repeatedly act disrespectfully should be told to leave the school. As a Tae Kwon Do instructor your school must serve as an example of what the ideals of the art are. People will judge more than just your school by the way you allow your students to conduct themselves. They will judge our art itself. While it is true that it is the tuition your students pay that allows you to keep your doors open, you should never ignore inappropriate behavior simply to keep students. You will find that your students, and the community, will respect you more if you maintain strict standards. In fact, you will probably find that you will attract more students by insisting on high behavior standards. They will understand that you care.

Rules of Conduct

Any well-run school establishes a set of rules for conduct within the *dojang.* These regulations establish a baseline for behavior by students and guests. By having a set policy of proper behavior, you are telling your students that the *dojang* is a place to be respected. As opposed to the eleven commandments of Tae Kwon Do, which outline general principles to help guide our actions, school rules are a list of specific behaviors that the students are expected to conform to. However, the students will only respect the rules and the school if you yourself do so. All Y. H. Park Taekwondo Centers have the same set of rules that students are expected to abide by. While there may be some slight differences between our rules and the rules of other Tae Kwon Do schools, these will give you a sense of the type of behavior that is expected inside the *dojang.*

1.   When you enter the *dojang,* salute by placing your right hand over your heart, then return it to your side and bow to: the *dojang* itself, your Master Instructor, your fellow students. Note that you do *not* place your hand over your heart when you bow to an indi-

vidual. Bowing is a means of showing respect. Anyone you bow to should return your bow. The bow should be slow and genuine, taking about six seconds. Do not look at the person you are bowing to—this shows that you trust the person and that he/she can trust you too.

2. If you arrive late for class, wait on your knees at the *dojang* entrance for permission from the Master to enter. Never leave class without the Master's permission.

3. The following are not allowed in the *dojang:* shoes, socks, gum chewing, loud laughter, bad language, arguing, rough-housing, unsupervised sparring, smoking or jewelry other than a smooth wedding ring. The *dojang* is a place of discipline. It must be treated with the respect worthy of a place of great honor—it is the place where you learn, develop, make friends and grow.

4. You must wear a clean, World Taekwondo Federation–approved uniform.

5. Whenever you approach your instructor, bow to him/her and wait for him to acknowledge your presence. Then speak politely in a quiet and respectful manner, remembering to end each sentence with "sir" or "ma'am."

6. When you need help ask your instructor. He/she will be happy to help. *Never* ask an instructor to demonstrate a technique. Simply explain what you do not understand and he/she will decide how to help you.

7. Always be as courteous as possible and obey your instructor. Advanced students should help to guide the lower belts by exemplifying proper behavior and encouraging the lower belts to do the same.

8. Do not demonstrate or teach Tae Kwon Do outside of your school without permission from the master of your school. Never degrade Tae Kwon Do, the reputation of your school, or any member or teacher of your school.

9. You must have the permission of your Master to participate in any competition or martial arts activity.

Just as there are rules of conduct for the students, certain things are expected of Tae Kwon Do instructors as well. As leaders within the Tae Kwon Do community, instructors are expected to teach and promote the art in a dedicated, patient and friendly manner. They should seek to foster the mental and physical growth of their students, encouraging good behavior, friendship and a positive attitude. They should act as mentors to their students and serve as examples of positive and moral living. In short, Tae Kwon Do instructors should strive to follow these guidelines:

To listen to and understand the needs and wants of your students
and their families and to address those needs and wants specifically.

To continually educate and train yourself and update your skills in
communication and instruction to maintain a commitment to ex-
cellence.

To educate and train your students so that they are empowered to
protect themselves and maintain optimal physical and mental
health.

To maintain a school environment that gives each individual student
the opportunity to pursue and achieve a greater level of personal
success and freedom.

COACHING

It is virtually impossible to be involved in Tae Kwon Do without also
being involved in tournament competition. Although not every stu-

dent will be interested in competition, if you
want to operate a successful school, you must
be able to provide the opportunity to compete
for those students who are interested. From a
marketing standpoint, a school that has numerous trophies displayed clearly conveys
the idea that students are being given quality
instruction. Further, competition can help to
forge strong bonds among the students in
your school, whether they themselves are
competing not. Few things build as profound
a feeling of camaraderie as cheering for someone from your own school as he or she pits
their skill against someone else. Win or lose,
a sense of pride will be felt by each of your students as they watch one
of their own in the ring.

Preparing students for competition is not very different from normal class instruction. After all, tournaments simply test the very things
that you have been teaching them. When a student expresses interest
in competition he or she needs to begin to focus more of the training
on the anticipated competition. Many schools offer specialty classes
where the bulk of the practice session is focused on fighting or forms.
Keep in mind, however, that while it is always good to win, it is the
development of the student's character as a competitor that is most important. Tournament competition should be an educational and
enjoyable aspect of a student's Tae Kwon Do experience. If your under-

lying motivation for having your students compete is the glorification of your school, however, you are doing them a disservice. Your students will also become aware that your focus is on yourself instead of them, and they will seek instruction from someone else.

Coaching Qualifications

As a coach you must strive to remain objective about yourself, especially your shortcomings. You cannot adequately prepare someone else for competition if you yourself are ignorant of certain physical, technical, professional or administrative aspects of the sport. Unfortunately, there are people who have little or no tournament experience themselves, yet represent themselves as coaches. If improperly prepared for competition, students will at the very least do poorly. In the worst case they can be seriously injured. Because of these reasons, certain procedures have been enacted by the WTF to ensure that coaches are in fact qualified to function in that role. While United States Taekwondo Union certification may not be necessary for you to enter your students in some local tournaments, we strongly urge anyone interested in putting together a team to take the USTU coaching clinic. It can only benefit you and your students. To be certified as a coach, the USTU requires that the person:

1.   possess a WTF dan (black belt) certificate;
2.   be at least 18 years of age;
3.   be a registered member of the USTU;
4.   successfully complete the USTU coaching clinic with a minimum score of 75.

Once earned, coach certification is valid for a period of 12 months. Along with ensuring that the coach is technically competent and up to date on all USTU regulations, certification also grants coaches special privileges at sanctioned tournaments. Specifically, certified coaches are allowed in the warm-up area of the competition as well as being able to coach his/her competitors from ringside.

Competition Categories

There are three categories of competition: forms (*poomse*), breaking (*kyuk pah*), and sparring (*kyorugi*). Contestants can register for one, two or all three events. Forms competition is a good way for students to learn how refined and precise their techniques are. During a forms competition, students perform one form before a panel of judges. They are judged on the correctness of each technique and the dynamic energy they put into the form as well as the correctness of the form itself (doing the right techniques in the right order).

Breaking competition is a good way for students to demonstrate their power and control of focus. There are no set requirements for breaking. Participants can do single or multiple breaks using any combination of techniques they like. To make the best impression on the judges, however, the more dynamic the technique the better. A simple side kick through a stack of boards, for example, will not impress the judges as much as breaking a lesser number of boards with a more difficult technique. Although most people stay with breaking boards, some people break other things such as brick, concrete and even slabs of ice. Generally, the organization hosting the tournament will provide guidelines for breaking competitions. Be aware that the USTU does *not* include breaking competitions as part of official tournaments, although most local tournament organizers do.

Sparring is where students pull all elements of their training together and put them to the test. Here speed, control, precision, timing and power have to be properly coordinated against a moving opponent. During these matches, competitors score points by landing punches and kicks against valid target areas on their opponent's body with enough force to visibly shake them. To make the matches as fair as possible, sparring competitions are separated into divisions according to age, weight and rank (see Appendix C). For competitors in the junior divisions (ages 13–18) kicks to the head are permitted only if done under control with light contact so that no injury results.

Tournaments

There are many levels of competition ranging from locally organized tournaments to WTF–sanctioned international championships. Local tournaments are competitions hosted by schools in your area. You should always exercise a degree of caution, however, before allowing your students to enter any local tournament. Although most tournament organizers model their competitions on USTU guidelines, since these tournaments do not fall under the jurisdiction of the USTU, the organizers do not have to adhere to all of the rules and regulations of a sanctioned competition. You want to be certain that the competition rules are ones that you approve of and that you are satisfied with the safety precautions. Although a local competition may not be formally sanctioned by the USTU, if you have evaluated it and find it to be sponsored by a legitimate and responsible host, a local tournament can be an excellent way for first-time competitors to get some experience in the ring.

USTU–sanctioned competitions are organized into three levels. State (and District) Association Championships compose the first level. The next level is comprised of the National Collegiate Taekwondo Championships and the U.S. Open Taekwondo Championships. The highest level is the annual National Taekwondo Championships. To compete in any of these tournaments, contestants must:

1. be a citizen of the United States of America;
2. possess a WTF rank certificate;
3. be a registered member of the USTU;
4. *not* be registered to participate or have participated as a professional athlete or coach in *any* sport,
5. *not* receive or have received any form of payment for their participation in a sports competition, unless granted special permission by the USTU or WTF;
6. *not* permit or have permitted their name or likeness to be used for advertising other than the promotion of Tae Kwon Do schools, tournaments or exhibitions;
7. not behave in a manner contradictory to the spirit of fair play.

To compete in the National Championships individuals must be among the top four winners (in their division) in any of the first or second level championships. Only those winners will receive invitations to the National Championships. To try out for a spot on the U.S. National Team, a person must have finished in the top four (in his/her division) of the National Championships. Trials for spots on the national team are held in two stages. The first level is conducted as a round robin competition—each competitor fights every other competitor in the division. The two persons with the highest scores qualify to move on to the finals. Approximately four to six weeks prior to an international tournament, the finalists will fight a series of matches. Whoever wins two out of three matches earns the spot on the team.

MANAGING THE BUSINESS

Technical ability and dedication are not enough. If you are serious about operating a Tae Kwon Do school as a business, there is one more thing you should do first—go to school. While it is not necessary to earn a master's degree in business administration, you can only benefit from taking courses in business management. Each year many competent and caring martial artists open schools, only to close them within 12 months because they could not generate sufficient revenue to keep their doors open. The overwhelming reason for the failure of these

schools has nothing to do with the qualifications of the instructors. Rather, they fail because the operators do not know how to manage a business. While this book is not intended to teach you all of the details of operating a business, we will outline some of the most important aspects of how to competently manage a Tae Kwon Do school.

Physical Layout

To manage a school, you must think of it as a service business. As such there are certain basic requirements that need to be met. Physically,

there should be a functional logic to the layout of your school. It should contain the following areas: a lobby, an office, the training area, a changing area, restrooms and a storage area. When people walk in the front door of the school, they enter the lobby. This is where they get their first impression. Make sure it is a favorable one. The lobby should be a clean, bright and welcoming place. We recommend that it be decorated in neutral colors so as not to detract from the *dojang,* the actual training area itself. Rank belts displayed on the wall here help set goals for the students. This is also a good place for your bulletin board and trophy case. It is also a good place to locate your "pro shop" display case. Throughout their training, students need to acquire and replace uniforms and equipment. Many martial arts suppliers give discounts to schools that buy in bulk. By having the equipment and supplies on hand that you want your students to use, you can encourage them to buy from your "pro shop" directly. Since you are able to purchase at a discount, you can supply your students with the materials they need at a competitive price while you make a small profit on the items yourself. Do not underestimate the importance of small fund-raising techniques such as this. They can help keep your business afloat.

The office should be located next to the lobby at the front of the school. This is where you talk to prospects, counsel students, hold meetings, do the books and perform any other business function. It should have a door for privacy when necessary, be neatly kept and professional-looking. By professional we mean neutral wall colors, simple furniture, perhaps a few pieces of tasteful artwork and school photographs. We strongly advise that you avoid pictures of violence and competition, as these may convey the wrong messages. On the wall behind your desk to one side is a good place to locate your training certificates, awards and any other documents that establish your credentials as an instructor. This will allow your visitors to examine your credentials as they speak to you, reinforcing the fact that you are a qualified instructor. Many offices also have a one-way mirror that allows the instructor to look out onto the training area without distracting the students. Your office should be positioned in a way that allows you to see everyone who enters and leaves the school. If a visitor appears in your lobby, warmly greet that person and find out how you can help. He or she may be a walk-in future student.

As for the training area itself, to accommodate a class of 50 students you will need a space approximately 25 feet wide and 70 feet long (1,750 square feet). Mirrors should be placed on the walls wherever it is convenient. Be aware that mirrors placed directly opposite each other create an infinite reflection effect that can be distracting. The walls themselves should be painted in a light, neutral color to give the space a bright atmosphere. Floor surface varies with individual taste. Some instructors prefer bare wood floors, while others favor padding or carpeting of some kind. Since you will probably not have your space built to your specifications, you may have to contend with a base flooring not designed for your needs, such as cement. Tightly woven indoor-outdoor carpeting of some dark, neutral color is sufficient for most school needs, although it will provide little protection against falls. If padding is installed under the carpet, it should not be too thick. You want to avoid having a spongy-feeling floor. This slows down movement and can result in students catching their feet or toes. Traditionally, the national flag, the Korean flag and the WTF flag are displayed in the training area.

The changing area should be located at the rear of the school. It should be equipped with lockers so that students can store clothes and personal items while in class. If possible, loops for personal padlocks or some other means of securing the lockers should be provided. While we like to think that our students will all get along and be completely trustworthy, there is always the possibility that a less than honest person may gain access in your school on occasion. Secure lockers protect against those opportunities. You may also wish to consider installing showers. This will help to attract adults in particular to your program. Remember, however, that this will also raise your costs, both in terms of initial construction and maintenance.

Restrooms should be decorated in pleasant colors and kept adequately stocked with soap and paper goods. Above all, you must be sure to **keep it clean.** A restroom's condition reflects on your school. Ideally, it should be located near the rear of the school, preferably close to the changing areas. While a unisex restroom may serve your needs, be aware that some local building codes require two restrooms.

The storage space should be located in an out-of-the-way area and kept locked. Whether it is to protect small children from poisonous cleaning solvents or to keep your valuable supplies from growing legs and walking away on their own, you should make sure that this space is secured. The small expense of installing a lock in the beginning will save you from problems later on.

You may not be able to design your school in this ideal way. The space you have may contain interferences such as support pillars or permanent walls. It may be square-shaped instead of rectangular. With some creativity, however, such obstacles can be overcome. Be sensible in your choice, however. No matter how great a bargain it might be, do not rent a space that cannot be made to serve your needs.

Hours of Operation

Once you have configured your space, you need to decide on your daily schedule. Most typical schools are open Monday to Friday from 10:00 A.M. to 9:00 P.M. and on Saturday from 9:00 A.M. to 1:00 P.M. Saturday afternoons and Sundays are excellent times for birthday parties and other promotional activities that can substantially increase the income of your school. Marketing, bookkeeping and any other administrative work is done when classes are not in session (typically between 9:00 A.M. and 3:00 P.M.). Many people make the mistake of assuming that the business is only open during actual class hours. One of the attractions for some is the belief that they can make a good income running a part-time business. This is a serious mistake. While you must be there to conduct classes, you cannot ignore the administrative functions. Once a school is established, many instructors hire an assistant to run much of the day-to-day functions. As the operator of a new school, however, you should expect to handle this yourself. Even if you do grow to the point where you need to hire someone, you should always have a hand in the administrative details. After all, it is your school. Nothing should be going on that you are not aware of.

When arranging your class schedule, you must take into consideration the different natures of your students. Classes for Mighty Mites (3–4 years of age) should be no more than 30 minutes long due to their limited attention span. All other classes are typically 45 to 50 minutes long. These include Pee-Wees (5–7), Children (8–14) and Adults (15 and above). A 10–15-minute break between classes allows you time to talk with your students and keep in touch with them. This is a very important time when you can discuss rank tests, private lessons and other activities.

The class schedule must be arranged so as to accommodate the needs of all students, both new and old, as the school grows. In general, classes for children are usually held in the afternoons, after school is over, and early on Saturday mornings. Classes for adults are held in the evenings, after most businesses close, and toward midday on Saturdays. A typical schedule might be arranged as follows:

CHILDREN

RANK	Mon.	Tues.	Wed.	Thurs.	Fri.	Sat.
White Yellow Orange	3:00 P.M.	5:00 P.M.	3:00 P.M.	5:00 P.M.	4:00 P.M.	9:00 A.M.
Green Blue Brown	4:00 P.M.	3:00 P.M.	4:00 P.M.	3:00 P.M.	4:00 P.M.	10:00 A.M.
High Br. Red High Red	5:00 P.M.	6:00 P.M.	5:00 P.M.	6:00 P.M.	5:00 P.M.	10:00 A.M.
Deputy & 1,2,3,4 Black Belt	6:00 P.M.	4:00 P.M.	6:00 P.M.	4:00 P.M.	5:00 P.M.	10:00 A.M.

ADULTS

	Mon.	Tues.	Wed.	Thurs.	Fri.	Sat.
White Yellow Orange	7:00 P.M.	8:00 P.M.	7:00 P.M.	8:00 P.M.	6:00 P.M.	11:00 A.M.
Green to Black	8:00 P.M.	7:00 P.M.	8:00 P.M.	7:00 P.M.	7:00 P.M.	11:00 A.M.

Notice that in the above example, the time for each session changes from day to day. This is to allow your students to choose the days and times that fit into their own daily schedules. Students will not attend classes if they are not held at times convenient for them. Although you are the ultimate authority in class, you are running a service business. As such, you must put some effort into accommodating their needs.

MARKETING

National statistics reveal that about 70 percent of the students in martial arts schools are children. The main body of your students will probably be between 4 and 14 years of age. Of these, approximately 65 percent will be boys and 35 percent girls. Young adult males up to 21 are the second largest group, followed by established adults, both male and female, up to about 45 years of age. The groups that provide the fewest students are girls from 16 to 20 years old and senior citizens of both sexes.

In order to attract students, however, potential students must first be aware of your school's existence. Your school must establish a visible presence within the community. One way to do this is by selecting the right location. We will assume that you are going to locate your business in a shopping center or strip mall. When selecting a location, the following list of questions should be considered. The more of these questions that you can answer with a "yes," the better your location is.

> Do you have a major discount, food or drug store in the same center as your school?
>
> Is your school in the main body of the center?
>
> Does your school face a street?
>
> Can your windows (and the classes inside) be seen from the street?
>
> Are there other businesses that draw large numbers of people from your target market (parents and children for the most part) in the center?
>
> Is the center accessible from both sides of the street?
>
> Is there a lot of parking available nearby?
>
> Is there access to public transportation nearby?
>
> Is there a major fast food chain in the center?
>
> Is your school the only full-time commercial martial arts school within a two-mile radius?
>
> Do you have a large marquee sign?
>
> Is your school surrounded by residential areas?
>
> Is there a major draw directly opposite your studio that would allow people to see your school as they leave?
>
> Is there an elementary or secondary school close to your location?
>
> Are you located within a middle-income area?

Once you have selected the right location, you must advertise your presence to the community. Experience has shown that the best advertising vehicles for martial arts schools are television (local and cable), radio (top 40 and easy listening), telemarketing, direct mail, "shopper/penny saver" type local newspapers, local magazines, the yellow pages, and lead boxes (this will be explained in more detail later). Although television and radio advertisements are some of the most effective vehicles, they are also the most costly. As a new school owner you probably will not have the financial resources to take advantage of them, so we will restrict our discussions to other venues.

In order to plan your advertising, you need to have a clear understanding of three critical factors: who your target audience is, where your potential students will come from, and what message you want your advertising to deliver. Unless you can answer these questions, your advertising will be undirected and ineffective. What you want from your ad campaign of course is future students. You want people to telephone you or walk into your school. While it is always desirable to spread awareness of your school, you must keep in mind that what you ultimately want from your ad campaign is *leads.* You want to make people approach you so that you can demonstrate to them that yours is the right martial art school for them.

As to exactly who your target audience is, that will vary depending on your situation. As the operator of a new school, you will probably want to cover the broadest spectrum possible. However, since the majority of your students will typically be children between 4 and 14 years, you will do well to focus a large part of your energies here. Remember that if your focus is to attract children, your advertising must also appeal to their parents, who enroll them and pay the tuition. Advertising to such a dual audience takes skill. You need to generate interest in the children to make them want to ask for lessons and at the same time present your school in a way that will make the parents see the lessons as beneficial for the development of their children.

As to where to locate potential students, it has been shown that people usually will only travel about five to seven miles for martial arts classes. This is one reason to be very careful in the selection of your location. If you are located too far out of the way, many people will not be willing to make the trip, no matter how magnificent your school may be. Since your students will be coming from areas within the immediate vicinity of your school, you should plan to keep your advertising local. This can benefit you in two ways. First, local advertising is relatively inexpensive, allowing you to generate a large volume of ads for a fairly low cost. Second, because you are focusing on such a small area, you can saturate the area with your advertising.

Finally, as to the message you want your advertising to convey, this will depend on the individual needs of your target audience. While it is simpler and less expensive to create one flyer (for direct mail advertising), creating different flyers to appeal to different target audiences is more effective. In general, kids want to have fun and do something "cool," while their parents want an activity that will benefit their children. Flyers to attract children for students should have pictures showing students having fun in class, while the text of the flyer should explain the physical and social benefits of Tae Kwon Do training. Older children and adults each have their own reasons for finding interest in the martial arts. Teens may want an activity that will increase their self-confidence, while adults may want something to get them in shape and relieve tension. Flyers for these groups should contain text and illustrations that emphasize those aspects of Tae Kwon Do training.

In general, we have found that the different needs and interests of potential students can be categorized with a high degree of accuracy based on the age of the potential student. Typically, Tae Kwon Do students can be classified into one of eight age range groups: young children (3–6), children (7–11), early teenagers (12–14), older teens (15–18), young adults (19–29), middle-aged adults (30–39), established adults (40–49) and seniors (50–70). Each age group tends to have certain specific traits that they share. However, each age group also tends to have distinct needs that can be addressed by Tae Kwon Do. The following chart identifies these needs and explains ways in which the practice of Tae Kwon Do can help people in each group.

3–6   Young children are working to develop their motor skills and social skills. Parents of these children are interested in helping them to build a strong foundation in these areas. Tae Kwon Do can help with the development of concentration, balance and coordination.

7–11   Older children are interacting more socially as they begin school. They are learning to know what they like and dislike. Parents often sense that their children need more attention than they receive in school. Tae Kwon Do can help with discipline, concentration and self-defense.

12-14   Early teenagers are entering a very difficult time in their lives. The onset of puberty often causes feelings of self doubt as they begin to compare themselves to others. Parents can be at a loss for how to help their children through this time. Tae Kwon Do can help by giving them a positive focus in their lives and by instilling in them a sense of discipline, respect, self-confidence and self-defense.

15–18   Older teens are often rebellious. They have clear tastes and ideas and are easily frustrated by having to obey the rules of their parents or other authority figures. They are children in adult bodies who desperately want to be adults. Parents are often overwhelmed by the moody changes in their children and want some way to ease their bitterness and frustration. Tae Kwon Do can help with discipline, respect, fitness, confidence and self-defense, as well as providing a constructive way to channel their energies.

19–29   Young adults tend to have an optimistic energy about them. They have reached adulthood and are looking for a challenge to focus their energies on. Tae Kwon Do can provide them with a challenge, physical fitness and self-defense.

30–39   Many middle-aged adults are often in low- to mid-level management positions. If they are parents, they have the additional responsibility of raising children. As a result people in this age range are often under considerable stress. Tae Kwon Do can provide them with sport, relaxation, confidence, fitness and self-defense.

40–49   Many established adults are dissatisfied with parts of their lives. They can feel that their lives did not turn out as they had planned and that they have little control to change things for the better at this point. Tae Kwon Do can help them with relaxation, fitness, weight control, stamina, strength and a new challenge. Developing self-defense abilities is not usually a major concern for people in this age group and up.

50–70   Seniors can be timid and lack confidence. They feel their physical abilities diminishing and want a way to revitalize themselves. Tae Kwon Do can help with relaxation, fitness, fun, confidence, and reviving the idea that it is not too late to do something new. An interesting corollary regarding this group is that as experienced adults their patience can be a great asset. Because they are some of the least physically strong, they are not able to "muscle" a technique. Therefore in order for their techniques to be effective they must do them properly. Since most seniors have retired from full-time work, they can usually put a lot of time into an activity and learn it well. This can make them some of the best students.

Once you have decided on your target audience(s), you can now begin to plan your advertising campaign. Its important to plan your advertising very carefully. Begin by drawing up a year's schedule. If things change, you can make revisions, but you will need a guide to start with. The schedule should show each newspaper or other medium you have decided on, the dates you intend to have your advertising appear and the associated cost. The exact format of your advertisement depends on your personal taste and budget. For print media, eye-catching graphics are wonderful, but the more extravagant your ad the more costly it will be. Avoid having so much going on in your ad that readers are confused.

It should attract their attention but be clear. Do not fill the ad or flyer with information about schedules, fees, your credentials or other details. Save that for face-to-face conversation. However, you *must* include the name, address and phone number of your school. If you need help, most advertisers have people who can assist you with creating your ad, although they will usually charge you for this service. You should include on your student enrollment form a question about how the student learned of your school. This will help you to concentrate your efforts on the most effective advertising media.

The Yellow Pages

An ad in the Yellow Pages is a must, but a simple listing of your school's name and phone number will do you no good at all. Unfortunately, there is so much competition for page space that you will probably not gain any advantage by investing heavily in a large ad either. You should take out an ad that is large enough to tell your story. Use the age group chart we included earlier to help you decide on the best format for your ad. List the advantages of enrolling in your school in an ad that is large enough to tell readers that you are alert to their needs and really want them for students. If your display is good, people will call you instead of the school with the largest ad.

Print Advertising

Newspapers are probably the first media that come to mind for print advertising. They reach people of all ages, income and education levels. Many papers also publish demographic versions or sections that are available only in certain areas. Since you don't need your advertising message to reach beyond the immediate area of your school, demographic editions can be a good choice.

Another good print medium is the "shopper/penny-saver" type paper that is either given away locally on stands or mailed. It costs little to advertise in these, and they reach the people you want. The most effective ad positions are of course the front and back covers, but be prepared to pay more for these choice places.

In print media, your message can be almost any length. Newspaper ads can also be changed often in response to your needs and usually bring quick responses. Since newspapers are divided into departments, you can tell the paper to run your ad where future students are most likely to see it.

Direct Mail

Direct mail means that you will be mailing your printed advertisement directly to a preselected target group of potential students and/or their parents. The typical self-mailer is a single 8 1/2-by-11-inch page that folds together in thirds with the mailing label, postage and return address on the outside. You can make use of the age group chart we included earlier to help create the appropriate flier for your target group. To locate potential students in your area who meet your target group you should contact a local mailing list house. You supply them with the profile of the people you want to contact and they will send you a printed list of labels that you can put directly on your fliers. For example, if you are interested in children as students, you would specify that you want a list of middle- to upper-income families in your area with children between the ages of 4 and 12. For a higher fee you can arrange for the house to label and mail your fliers for you. You can also get the list on diskette. However, keep in mind that this type of information gets out of date quickly. Mailing your fliers is relatively inexpensive since you pay bulk-rate postage. But be aware that bulk postage can take as long as three weeks to be delivered.

You can expect a 1.5 to 3 percent response rate from direct mail, or about 15 to 30 calls for every 1,000 fliers. To get the best possible response to your ads, we recommend that you send the same flier three times to the people on your list at three-week intervals. We have found that the best time of year to do your mailing is at the end of summer, just as school is beginning. Right after the new year is another good time to do direct mail.

Lead Boxes

Lead boxes are one of the most cost-efficient ways to advertise your school. A lead box is a box placed inside a nearby business with a registration pad and a sign behind it that announces a contest. The prize is usually an introductory offer to your school. Once people have placed their names and addresses in the box, you award them with a free week of lessons. You are leading them to your school, hence the name "lead box." Try to make your box as colorful and distinctive as possible to attract attention. Above all, it should look professional. Its construction must be neat and the lettering and illustrations clear. On the back of the box you should display the name and telephone number of your school. Of course, some people who fill out the slip of paper aren't really interested. But if a lead box brings you one new member per week, ten of them can generate as much as 520 new members a year!

You should try to put out at least 25 to 30 lead boxes within a two-mile radius around your school. You should select businesses whose patrons may have an interest in martial arts. The following is a list of good places to put lead boxes: supermarkets, health food stores, restaurants, sporting goods stores, doctor's/dentist's offices, fast food restaurants, clothing stores, pharmacies, local strip malls, convenience stores, small retail stores, beauty salons, auto parts stores, dry cleaners, donut shops, racquetball/tennis clubs, ice cream stores, night clubs, supervised launderettes, home repair shops, hardware stores, shoe stores, banks.

Once you have identified the stores where you want to place your boxes, approach the store's manager or owner directly. If possible, enlist the aid of people who are patrons of the store. The manager will be more receptive to someone he knows. Explain to the manager that the boxes are for a membership drive and say that you want to offer his customers a chance to win martial arts lessons. Tell him that the box will be serviced weekly and that he has no responsibility for it. Assure him that the box will be replaced at once if it becomes worn or unsightly. Be sure to show him your school's name and phone number on the back so that he can contact you if necessary. If he agrees, ask the manager where he wants you to place the box and be sure to thank him!

You should check your lead boxes at least once a week and send out award certificates promptly. About 10 to 15 percent of the people who get the certificates will respond within four days. Follow-up phone calls can increase the response rate by 3 to 5 percent.

Telemarketing

Telemarketing is another way to reach the people whose names you obtained from your lead boxes or mailing list. Before you make your call, you should have a set script rehearsed so that you do not hesitate or leave out any important information. When you call, remember that your objective is to get the prospective student to come out to your school for a free week of lessons. You should keep the following factors in mind when making these calls. First, you only have about fifteen seconds to capture the person's attention. Since you are interrupting them, get to the point fast. Don't be short, but don't ramble on either. Keep your approach light and positive and don't forget your manners. If you try to strong-arm people, they will hang up. Your tone should be confident, enthusiastic and professional. Be cheerful and smile when you talk, even though the other person cannot see you. The prospective student will sense your attitude and respond to it. Do not hesitate or sound bored. This will project a negative image of you and your school. *Speak clearly.* Never chew gum or eat while talking on the phone. If the prospective student asks about prices, be honest, but don't get involved in a long conversation about price. Remind him or her that you are calling to give them a free week's worth of lessons with no obligation on their part. Be sure to tell the prospective student to ask for you personally when coming in. This will make the individual feel more at ease. Whether or not prospective students accept your offer for free lessons, be courteous and thank them for their time—they may change their minds or refer friends to your school.

APPENDIX A
Rules of Competition

RING DIMENSIONS

For all international competitions, the dimensions of the contest are to measure 8 square meters (26 square feet), with the outer boundary measuring 12 square meters (39 square feet). The surface of the competition area must be flat and covered with WTF-approved foam padding or wood.

For regional and local tournaments the dimensions of the contest area are to measure 6 square meters (19 1/2 square feet), with the outer boundary measuring 8 square meters (26 square feet).

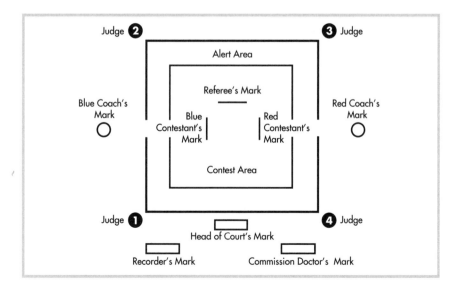

Uniform and Safety Equipment

All contestants are required to wear a clean, WTF-approved uniform in good condition. Contestants are also required to wear WTF-approved headgear, chest protector, forearm and shin pads. Men must wear a protective groin cup. Only the headgear and chest protector may be worn outside of the uniform. All other protective padding must be worn inside the uniform. To differentiate between competitors in the ring, one will wear a red (*hong*) chest protector and the other will wear a blue (*chung*) chest protector.

Competitors are expected to keep both themselves and their uniforms clean. Unsatisfactory personal hygiene will result in disqualification of the violator. Nails must be cut short (both hand and foot). Long hair must be securely tied back. Metal objects (jewelry) and eyeglasses may not be worn during competition. A maximum of two layers of tape is permitted in the case of injury when the tournament physician approves its use. Competitors may not wear a splint or a cast.

The use of nonprescribed drugs or intoxicants by competitors either before or during a match will result in the disqualification of the violator.

Valid Targets

The only targets allowed in competition are on the front of the body between the competitor's waist and base of the neck, but *not* the throat itself. The only body surfaces that can be used to score points are the forefist (open-handed techniques are prohibited) and any part of the foot below the ankle. Hand techniques may not be directed to the face, however foot techniques are permitted to the head. For junior divisions (ages 13–18) kicks to the head *must* be made with light contact and executed with complete control without causing injury or a penalty will be invoked. Each hit will earn a competitor one point providing that the strike was executed with the proper technique, balance and power. In order to score a point, a technique must land against an authorized area of an opponent's body with sufficient force to cause a visible shock to the body.

Strikes to valid target areas will not be awarded points if the competitor loses balance after completing the attack, if the competitor is holding the opponent during the attack, or if the competitor continues to attack during a clinch.

Strikes to nontarget areas will not be awarded points. Depending on the severity of the offense, a competitor may receive a half point deduction, a full point deduction, or be disqualified.

Officials

All competitions are to be supervised by the following WTF-certified officials: one referee, four judges, at least one juror, a timekeeper, a weigher and a recorder.

Referee duties:

1. To oversee and control the competition.
2. To inspect all competitors before matches.
3. To provide competition rules, declare the beginning and end of matches and to give warnings and instructions to competitors.
4. To announce deducted points, announce disqualifications, signal invalid scores and control all activity in the ring.
5. To oversee the safety of the competitors.
6. To signal stops of the time clock.
7. To collect and submit judges' scorecards at the conclusion of each match.
8. To provide opinions to juror requests about judges' decisions.
9. To stop a match (during junior competitions) to consult judges regarding considerations of mismatch and technical knockouts. Such decisions require unanimous agreement by all judges, along with jury verification.

Judge duties:

1. To be positioned at each corner of the competition ring and assist the referee as necessary.
2. To advise the referee of invalid violation calls.
3. To note all warnings, points, rule infractions and disqualifications on the scorecard.
4. To total scores and indicate match winners on the scorecard.
5. To give completed scorecards to the referee following the end of each match.

Juror duties:

1. To consult with judges and the referee whenever necessary.
2. To review scorecards for consistency, accuracy and signatures of judges, and to bring questions regarding any of the aforementioned to the attention of the judges and/or referee.
3. To determine the winner of a match based on the scorecards of the judges and referee.
4. To request the replacement of judges or referees when the performance of these individuals is in question.
5. To sign and submit judges' and referee's scorecards to the tournament committee in the event of a protest for the rendering of a final decision.

Timekeeper duties:

> To start and stop the official clock and the referee's instructions and to announce the end of official time periods.

Recorder duties:

> To keep the official records of the results of each contest.

Weigher duties:

> To determine the weight of each competitor in the presence of a designated, certified referee.

DEFINITIONS

Knockdown:

1. Whenever any part of the body other than the competitor's feet touches the floor as the result of an attack.
2. Whenever a competitor is caused to stagger as the result of an attack.
3. Whenever a competitor bends over or squats without showing the intention to continue the match.

Knockout:

> Whenever a contestant cannot continue the match after the referee has completed a count of ten *(yol)*.

Stopped contest:

1. Whenever the referee or tournament physician determines that a contestant should not continue.
2. Whenever a competitor's coach throws a towel to stop the match.
3. Whenever a competitor protests a referee's call and fails to continue the match within one minute of the referee's command.

DECISIONS

The winner of a match is determined after considering each of the following criteria:

1. The disqualification of the opponent.
2. The withdrawal of the opponent.
3. The injury of the opponent due to a valid attack.

4. The knockout of the opponent due to a valid attack.
5. The difference in points.
6. The deduction of points during a match.
7. Considerations of superiority (see below).
8. Referee stops the contest.

RULES OF SUPERIORITY

In situations in which the match results in a tie score, the winner will be decided based on considerations of superiority. The most effective scoring techniques (best single techniques) executed by each competitor are compared and rated according to the following criteria:

1. A technique of sufficient power to result in an eight-count knockdown is considered superior to any other technique.
2. Any foot technique is considered superior to any hand technique.
3. Any jumping kick is considered superior to any standing technique.
4. Any kick to the head is considered superior than any kick to the body.
5. Any counterattack is considered superior to any initiated attack.
6. If the above criteria cannot resolve the tie, the more aggressive fighter is considered superior.

APPENDIX B
Referee Signals

Of all the officials presiding at a competition, the referee is the most visible. He controls everything that takes place within the ring. The various gestures he uses signal to the other officials as well as to the audience any important actions transpiring during a competition. Over the past several years the World Taekwondo Federation has modified the referee's hand signals in an effort to make them as clear and simple as possible. Whereas previously referees would make different gestures for each specific infraction, offenses are now grouped into four general categories: touching acts, negative acts, attacking acts, and undesirable acts. One signal now serves to identify those actions that fall under each of the above categories. The following signals are those now being used in all official Tae Kwon Do competitions, including the Olympics.

STARTING THE MATCH

Calling the Contestants:
The referee will extend the index fingers of both hands and spread his arms outward and down toward each contestants' starting marks, blue (*chung*) first and then red (*hong*).

Attention:

The referee will call the contestants to attention by saying, "*Cha-ryot,*" (attention) while lifting both hands to face height with palms facing toward each other. He will then have the competitors bow to each other by saying, "*Kyong-ye,*" (bow) as he lowers his palms to the floor so that his fingertips are almost touching and his hands are in front of his chest.

Ready:

The referee will have the competitors adopt fighting stances by calling, "*Joonbi,*" (ready) as he steps into a front stance and drops his right hand between the chests of the competitors in a knife-hand position. His left hand will be clenched and held down at his side.

Begin:

The referee will start the match by drawing back his lead foot as he brings both hands quickly together in front of his body with the palms facing each other. As he does this he will say, "*Si jak,*" (begin).

STOPPING THE MATCH

To stop the match for any reason, the referee will drop his right hand between the contestants in a knife-hand position as he says either, "*Kalyeo,*" (break), or "*Gu-mahn,*" (stop).

TIME OUT

The referee will first point to the Recorder with the index finger of his right hand. Then he will make an X by crossing both index fingers before his face as he says, "*Shi-gan,*" (time out).

10-SECOND COUNT

In the event of a knockdown, the referee will move to within one meter of the downed competitor and count from *hana* to *yol* (one to ten) in one-second intervals, extending one finger at a time.

RESUMING THE MATCH

To continue the match, the referee will quickly withdraw his hand from between the contestants to a position beside his ear as he says, "*Kae-sok*" (continue).

DECLARING THE WINNER

The referee will turn toward the winner and make either of the following gestures. If blue (*chung*) is the winner, he will extend his right arm upward at a 45° angle with his hand palm up in a knife-hand position as he says, "*Chung sung,*" (blue wins). If red (*hong*) is the winner, he will extend his left hand in a similar manner and say, "*Hong sung,*" (red wins).

HALF-POINT DEDUCTION

If a competitor performs an illegal act, the referee will pause the match. Once the competitors have stopped, he will bring his right hand to his left shoulder and then extend his arm to point at the violator with his index finger. Following this he will then make one of the four illegal act gestures and say either, "*Chung kyong-go,*" (blue penalty) or, "*Hong kyong-go,*" (red penalty).

FULL-POINT DEDUCTION

For severe infractions, the referee will first pause the match. When the competitors have stopped, he will bring his right hand to his left shoulder then extend his arm to point at the violator with his index finger. Next, he will raise his hand above his head with his finger pointing straight into the air. He will then make one of the illegal act gestures and say either, "*Chung gam-jeum*" (blue point deduction) or, "*Hong gam-jeum,*" (red point deduction).

ILLEGAL ACTS

Touching Acts:

Holding his right hand open in a knife-hand position, the referee will place the tips of his fingers to his left shoulder.

Negative Acts:

While clenching both hands into fists with palms down, the referee will bring the knuckles of his hands together twice in front of his chest.

Attacking Acts:

The referee will hold his left hand open in a knife-hand position with the fingertips pointing up and the thumb toward his shoulder as he strikes the palm with his right fist.

Undesirable Acts:

The referee will extend the index finger of his right hand and hold it up in front of his closed mouth.

APPENDIX C
Weight and Belt Divisions

SENIOR DIVISIONS
(AGE 17 AND ABOVE)

Weight class	Males	Females
Fin	below 54 kg. (119 lbs.)	below 47 kg. (103 lbs.)
Fly	54–58 kg. (119–128 lbs)	47–51 kg. (103–112 lbs.)
Bantam	58–62 kg. (128–136 lbs.)	51–55 kg. (112–121 lbs.)
Feather	62–67 kg. (136–147 lbs.)	55–59 kg. (121–130 lbs.)
Light	67–72 kg. (147–158 lbs.)	59–63 kg. (130–139 lbs.)
Welter	72–78 kg. (158–172 lbs.)	63–67 kg. (139–147 lbs.)
Middle	78–84 kg. (172–185 lbs.)	67–72 kg. (147–158 lbs.)
Heavy	above 84 kg. (185 lbs.)	above 72 kg. (158 lbs.)

JUNIOR DIVISIONS
BLACK BELT: AGES 14–17

Weight class	Males	Females
Fin	below 45 kg. (99 lbs.)	Below 42 kg. (93 lbs.)
Fly	45–48 kg. (99–106 lbs.)	42–44 kg. (93–97 lbs.)
Bantam	48–51 kg. (106–112 lbs.)	44–46 kg. (97–101 lbs.)
Feather	51–55 kg. (112–121 lbs.)	46–49 kg. (101–108 lbs.)
Light	55–59 kg. (121–130 lbs.)	49–52 kg. (108–115 lbs.)
Welter	59–63 kg. (130–139 lbs.)	52–55 kg. (115–121 lbs.)
Light–Middle	63–68 kg. (139–150 lbs.)	55–59 kg. (121–130 lbs.)
Middle	68–73 kg. (150–161 lbs.)	59–63 kg. (130–139 lbs.)
Light–Heavy	73–78 kg. (161–172 lbs.)	63–68 kg. (139–150 lbs.)
Heavy	above 78 kg. (172 lbs.)	Above 68 kg. (150 lbs.)

COLOR BELTS: AGES 16–17

Weight class	Males	Females
Fin	below 48 kg. (105 lbs.)	below 45 kg. (100 lbs.)
Fly	48–52 kg. (105–115 lbs.)	45–50 kg. (100–110 lbs.)
Bantam	52–57 kg. (115–125 lbs.)	50–55 kg. (110–120 lbs.)
Feather	57–61 kg. (125–135 lbs.)	55–59 kg. (120–130 lbs.)
Light	61–66 kg. (135–145 lbs.)	59–64 kg. (130–140 lbs.)
Welter	66–70 kg. (145–155 lbs.)	64–68 kg. (140–150 lbs.)
Middle	70–75 kg. (155–165 lbs.)	68–73 kg. (150–160 lbs.)
Heavy	above 75 kg. (165 lbs.)	above 73 kg. (160 lbs.)

COLOR BELTS: AGES 14–15

Weight class	Males	Females
Fin	below 43 kg. (95 lbs.)	below 42 kg. (92 lbs.)
Fly	43–48 kg. (95–105 lbs.)	42–46 kg. (92–102 lbs.)
Bantam	48–52 kg. (105–115 lbs.)	46–51 kg. (102–112 lbs.)
Feather	52–57 kg. (115–125 lbs.)	51–55 kg. (112–122 lbs.)
Light	57–61 kg. (125–135 lbs.)	55–60 kg. (122–132 lbs.)
Welter	61–66 kg. (135–145 lbs.)	60–65 kg. (132–142 lbs.)
Middle	66–70 kg. (145–155 lbs.)	65–69 kg. (142–152 lbs.)
Heavy	above 70 kg. (155 lbs.)	above 69 kg. (152 lbs.)

BLACK BELT AND COLOR BELTS: AGES 12–13

Weight class	Males	Females
Fin	below 39 kg. (85 lbs.)	below 37 kg. (82 lbs.)
Fly	39–43 kg. (85–95 lbs.)	37–42 kg. (82–92 lbs.)
Bantam	43–48 kg. (95–105 lbs.)	42–46 kg. (92–102 lbs.)
Feather	48–52 kg. (105–115 lbs.)	46–51 kg. (102–112 lbs.)
Light	52–57 kg. (115–125 lbs.)	51–55 kg. (112–122 lbs.)
Heavy	above 57 kg. (125 lbs.)	above 55 kg. (122 lbs.)

BLACK BELTS AND COLOR BELTS: AGES 10–11

Weight class	Males	Females
Fin	below 34 kg. (75 lbs.)	below 33 kg. (72 lbs.)
Fly	34–39 kg. (75–85 lbs.)	33–37 kg. (72–82 lbs.)
Bantam	39–43 kg. (85–95 lbs.)	37–42 kg. (82–92 lbs.)
Feather	43–48 kg. (95–105 lbs.)	42–46 kg. (92–102 lbs.)
Light	48–52 kg. (105–115 lbs.)	46–51 kg. (102–112 lbs.)
Heavy	above 52 kg. (115 lbs.)	above 51 kg. (112 lbs.)

BLACK BELT AND COLOR BELTS: AGES 8–9

Weight class	Males	Females
Fin	below 30 kg. (65 lbs.)	below 28 kg. (62 lbs.)
Fly	30–34 kg. (65–75 lbs.)	28–33 kg. (62–72 lbs.)
Bantam	34–39 kg. (75–85 lbs.)	33–37 kg. (72–82 lbs.)
Feather	39–43 kg. (85–95 lbs.)	37–42 kg. (82–92 lbs.)
Light	43–48 kg. (95–105 lbs.)	42–46 kg. (92–102 lbs.)
Heavy	above 48 kg. (105 lbs.)	above 46 kg. (102 lbs.)

BLACK BELT AND COLOR BELTS: AGES 6–7

Weight class	Males	Females
Fin	below 25 kg. (55 lbs.)	below 24 kg. (52 lbs.)
Fly	25–27 kg. (55–60 lbs.)	24–26 kg. (52–57 lbs.)
Bantam	27–32 kg. (60–70 lbs.)	26–30 kg. (57–67 lbs.)
Feather	32–36 kg. (70–80 lbs.)	30–35 kg. (67–77 lbs.)
Light	36–41 kg. (80–90 lbs.)	35–40 kg. (77–87 lbs.)
Heavy	above 41 kg. (90 lbs.)	above 40 kg. (87 lbs.)

APPENDIX D
Tae Kwon Do Governing Bodies

SANCTIONED NATIONAL TAE KWON DO ORGANIZATIONS

African Region:
Fédération Beninoise de Taekwondo
Fédération Burkinabe de Taekwondo
Cameroun Taekwondo Association
Congo Taekwondo Association
Taekwondo Federation of Côte d'Ivoire
The Egyptian Taekwondo Federation
Taekwondo Association of Ethiopia
Association Gabonaise de Taekwondo
Ghana Taekwondo Federation
The Kenya Taekwondo Association
Lesotho Taekwondo Association
The Taekwondo Association of Liberia
Libyan Taekwondo Federation
Association Malienne de Taekwondo
The Malagasy Federation of Taekwondo
Mauritius Taekwondo Association
Fédération Royal Marocaine de Taekwondo
Taekwondo Association of Nigeria
Sierra Leone Taekwondo Association
South African Association for Taekwondo
Sudanese General Association for Taekwondo
Swaziland National Martial Arts Association
Tanzania Taekwondo Association
Fédération Tunisienne de Karaté et des Disciplines Associées

Uganda Taekwondo Association
Fédération Zairoise de Taekwondo

Asian Region:
Afgan Taekwondo Federation
Australian Taekwondo Association
Bahrain Taekwondo Association
Bhutan Taekwondo Federation
Brunei State Taekwondo Association
Chinese Taipei Amateur Taekwondo Association
Fiji Taekwondo Association
Guam Taekwondo Federation
Hong Kong Taekwondo Association
Taekwondo Federation of India
Indonesian Taekwondo Federation
Taekwondo Federation of the Islamic Republic of Iran
The Iraqi Taekwondo Federation
Israel Taekwondo Federation
Japan Taekwondo Federation
Jordan Taekwondo Federation
Taekwondo Federation of the Republic of Kazakhstan
Taekwondo Federation of the Republic of Kirghizstan
Korean Taekwondo Association
Kuwait Judo and Taekwondo Federation
Lebanese Taekwondo Federation
Macao Taekwondo Association

Malaysia Taekwondo Association
Mongolian Taekwondo Federation
Myanmar Taekwondo Federation
Nepal Taekwondo Association
New Zealand Taekwondo Federation
Ligue de Karaté et Taekwondo de Nouvelle-
    Calédonie
Pakistan Taekwondo Federation
Papua New Guinea World Taekwondo Asso-
    ciation
The Philippine Taekwondo Association
Qatar Taekwondo Association
Samoa Taekwondo Association
Saudi Arabian Karate, Taekwondo and Judo
    Federation
Singapore Taekwondo Federation
Solomon Islands Taekwondo Association
Sri Lanka Taekwondo Association
Syrian Karate and Taekwondo Federation
Tadzhikistan Taekwondo Association
Fédération Tahitienne de Karaté, Taek-
    wondo, Kung-fu et Arts Martiaux
    Affinitaires
Thai Taekwondo Association
Tonga Taekwondo Association
Uzbekistan Taekwondo Association
Vietnam Taekwondo Association
Yemen Taekwondo Federation

European Region:
Federación Andorrana de Taekwondo
Armenian Taekwondo Federation
Austrian Taekwondo Federation
Taekwondo Federation of the Republic of Be-
    larus
Taekwondo Federation of Bosnia and Herze-
    govina
Union National Belge de Taekwondo
The British Taekwondo Control Board
Bulgarian Taekwondo Federation
Croatian Taekwondo Federation
Cyprus Judo, Karate and Taekwondo Federation
Dansk Taekwondo Forbund
The Finnish Taekwondo Federation

Fédération Française de Karaté, Taekwondo
    et Arts Martiaux Affinitaires
Deutsche Taekwondo Union
Hellenique Taekwondo Federation
Hungarian WTF Taekwondo Association
Taekwondo Council of Iceland
Irish Taekwondo Union
Federazione Italiana Taekwondo
Latvian Taekwondo Federation
Lithuanian Taekwondo Federation
Fédération Luxembourgeoise des Arts Martiaux
Taekwondo Federation of the Republic of
    Moldova
Taekwondo Bond Netherland
Norway Budo Federation
Polish Sport Taekwondo Federation
Federaçao Portuguesa de Taekwondo
Romanian Union of Taekwondo Clubs
Russian Taekwondo Union
Slovenian Taekwondo Association
Federación Española de Taekwondo
Swedish Budo Federation Taekwondo Com-
    mittee
Sektion Taekwondo Schweizerisher
Taekwondo Federation of Turkey
Ukrainian Taekwondo Federation
Yugoslavia Taekwondo Federation

Pan-American Region:
Confederación Argentina de Taekwondo
Aruba Taekwondo Association
Barbados Taekwondo Association
Bermuda Taekwondo Association
Federación Boliviana de Taekwondo
Confederaçao Brasileira de Taekwondo
WTF Taekwondo Association of Canada
Cayman Islands Taekwondo Federation
Federación Chilena de Taekwondo
Federación Colombiana de Taekwondo
Asociación Costarricense de Taekwondo
Cuban Taekwondo Federation
Federación Dominicana de Taekwondo
Federación Ecuadoriana de Taekwondo
Federación Salvadoreña de Taekwondo

National Taekwondo Federation of
    Guatemala
Guyana Taekwondo Association
Taekwondo Union of Haiti
Honduran Taekwondo Federation
Jamaican Taekwondo Association
Federación Mexicana de Taekwondo
Netherlands Antilles Taekwondo Associa-
    tion
Asociación Nicaragüense de Taekwondo
Comisión Panameña de Taekwondo
Confederación Paraguaya de Taekwondo
Federación de Taekwondo de Puerto Rico
Comisión Nacional de Taekwondo del Perú
St. Vincent and the Grenadines Taekwondo
    Association
Suriames Taekwondo Associatie
Republic of Trinidad & Tobago Taekwondo
    Association
United States Taekwondo Union
Federación Uruguaya de Taekwondo
Federación Venezolana Taekwondo
The Virgin Islands Taekwondo Federation

SANCTIONED INTERNATIONAL TAE KWON DO COMPETITIONS

African Games
Asian Games
Bolivarian Games
Central American and Caribbean Games
Olympic Games
Pan-American Games
South American Games
Southeast Asian Games
South Pacific Games

CONTACT ADDRESSES

The World Taekwondo Federation
President: Dr. Un-Yong Kim
Address: 635 Yuksam-Dong, Kangnam-Ku
Seoul, Korea
Telephone: 82.2.566-2505
Web site: www.wtf.or.kr/home.htm

The United States Taekwondo Union
President: Mr. Sang Chul Lee
Address: One Olympic Plaza, Suite 405
Colorado Springs, CO 80909
Telephone: (719) 578-4632
Web site: www.ustu.com

Y. H. Park Taekwondo Centers, Inc.
Owner: Grandmaster Y. H. Park
Address: 2343 Hempstead Turnpike
East Meadow, New York 11554
Telephone: (516) 735-3434

APPENDIX E
Promotion Requirements

Rank	Minimum Training Time	Required Form	Minimum age
1st Dan	one year	Tae Geuk 1–8	15/below 15*
1st Dan to 2nd Dan	one year	Koryo	16/15*
2nd Dan to 3rd Dan	two years	Kumgong	18/16*
3rd Dan to 4th Dan	three years	Taebek	21/18*
4th Dan to 5th Dan	four years	Pyung Won or Ship Jin	25/22*
5th Dan to 6th Dan	five years	Ship Jin or Ji Tae	30
6th Dan to 7th Dan	six years	Ji Tae or Chun Kwon	36
7th Dan to 8th Dan	eight years	Han Soo	44
8th Dan to 9th Dan	nine years	Ill Yo	53
9th Dan to 10th Dan	Decision by the Kukkiwon Promotion Commission		60

* If a student is awarded a Junior Black Belt (below age 15), they will be granted reduced age limits up to 5th Dan.

TAE KWON DO TERMINOLOGY

Unlike languages such as Japanese and Chinese, which are written using ideograms (picture-characters that each represent complete words or ideas), the Korean language is written using an alphabet. Known as *han-gul*, the characters that form the Korean alphabet each represent certain vowel and consonant sounds, allowing them to be combined in an almost limitless variety to create the words of this rich language. However, the Korean language uses some sound combinations not common to English. As a result, representing Korean words using Roman letters often leads to differences in "correct" spelling. In a dozen books about Korea you can find as many different ways to spell many of the same words. In writing these books we have tried to reflect the phonetic characteristics of the Korean words in our spelling.

HAN-GŬL (한글)

Consonants:

ㄱ	ㄴ	ㄷ	ㄹ	ㅁ	ㅂ	ㅅ
k/g	n	t/d	r/l	m	p/b	s/sh

ㅇ	ㅈ	ㅊ	ㅋ	ㅌ	ㅍ	ㅎ
ng	ch/j	ch′	k′	t′	p′	h

Vowels:

ㅏ	ㅑ	ㅓ	ㅕ	ㅗ	ㅛ	ㅜ	ㅠ	ㅡ	ㅣ
a	ya	ŏ	yŏ	o	yo	u	yu	ŭ	i

260

ANATOMY

ahpchook: ball of foot
baal: foot
baaldung: instep
dari: leg
dwi-chook: heel
eolgul: face
huri: waist
ip: mouth
joomock: fist
mok: neck
mo-li: head
momtong: body
moo-rup: knee
palkoop: elbow
palmock: wrist
pol: arm
son: hand
son-kut: fingertip
sonmock: wrist

BLOCKS

ahn maggi: inner arm block
ahn palmok pakhag maggi: outer arm block
ahre maggi: down block
backat maggi: outer block
eolgul maggi: face block (rising block)
han sonnal maggi: knife-hand block
hecho maggi: spreading block
kawi-u maggi: scissors block
kumkang maggi: diamond block
maggi: block
momtong maggi: middle block
narae maggi: double block
noollo maggi: groin block
pakhag maggi: reverse outer arm block
patang-son maggi: palm block

santil maggi: mountain block
son-nal maggi: single knife-hand block
ur-santil maggi: partial mountain block
wee maggi: high block
yeot pero maggi: X block

COMMANDS

barro: return (to previous position)
ba-quo: switch
cha-ryot: attention/come to attention
dorra: about face
gu-mahn: hold/stop
joonbi: ready/get ready
kae sok: continue
kalyeo: break
kyong-ye: bow
si-jak: begin/start

DIRECTIONS

ahn: in/inner
ahp: front
ahre: low
backat: out/outer
dolryo: round
dwi: back
gaunde: middle
gullgi: hook/hooking
hecho: spread/spreading
nare: double
o-ruen: right
tol gae: spin
wee: high
wen: left
yop: side

KICKS

ahp-bodo olligi: front rising kick

ahp cha-gi: front snap kick
ahp-jillo cha-gi: front thrust kick
bandul cha-gi: crossing kick
chik-gi: axe kick
dolryo cha-gi: round kick
dwi cha-gi: back kick
huryo cha-gi: hook kick
mil-ya cha-gi: pushing kick
moo-rup chi-gi: knee strike
narae cha-gi: double kick
tol gae cha-gi: spinning kick
yo-cha-gi: jumping kick
ye tan cha-gi: flying kick
yop-bodo olligi: side rising kick
yop cha-gi: side snap kick
yop-jillo cha-gi: side thrust kick

MOVEMENTS

cha-gi: kick/kicking
chi-gi: strike/striking
hecho: spread/spreading
jirugi: thrust/thrusting
jupgi: hold/holding
kyorugi: spar/sparring
maggi: block/blocking
modoo: gather/gathering
ye tan: fly/flying
yo: jump/jumping

NUMBERS

Counting

hanna: one
dul: two
set: three
net: four
dasot: five
yasot: six
elgub: seven
yodol: eight

ahob: nine
yol: ten

Listing

el: first
e: second
sam: third
sa: fourth
oh: fifth
yuk: sixth
chil: seventh
pul: eighth
koo: ninth
sib: tenth

STANCES

ahp-gubi sogi: forward stance
ahp sogi: walking stance
bum sogi: tiger stance
cha-ryot sogi: attention stance
dwi-gubi sogi: back stance
juchoom-sogi: horseback riding stance
koa-sogi: twisted stance
po jumok sogi: containing the vital energy stance
pyong-hi sogi: ready stance
sogi: stance

STRIKES

agwi-son chi-gi: arc-hand strike
ap-joomok chirugi: jab punch
bam joomok chi-gi: knuckle protruding strike
batang-son chi-gi: palm-heel strike
chirugi: forward strike (punch)

dung-joomock chi-gi: back-fist strike
huryo cha-gi: hook punch
kawi son-kut chi-gi: scissors fingertip strike
kom son chi-gi: bear-hand strike
me-joomok chi-gi: hammer-fist strike
palkoop chi-gi: elbow strike
paro chirugi: reverse punch
patang-son chigi: palm strike
pyon-joomock chi-gi: knuckle-fist strike
pyon son-kut chi-gi: spear-fingers strike
son-nal chi-gi: knife-hand strike
son-nal dung chi-gi: ridge-hand strike
tol chi-gi: square punch
yop chirugi: side punch

TITLES

bae sim: juror
bu sim: judge
chokyonim: instructor (first to third degree black belt)
joo sim: referee
kae sim: timekeeper
ki rohk: recorder
kwanjangnim: grand master instructor (seventh to ninth degree black belt)
sabomnin: master (fourth to six degree black belt)

GENERAL TERMS

ahn-nyong: hello
ahn-nyonghi gasipsiyo: good-bye (to the one who leaves)

ahn-nyonghi gesipsiyo: good-bye (to the one who stays)
ahn-nyong hasimnika: how are you?
baro-angi: lotus position
chonmaney: you are welcome
dan: rank (for black belts)
do: martial art/moral culture/way of life
dobok: Tae Kwon Do uniform
dojang: Tae Kwon Do gymnasium
donzigi: throw/throwing
gam-jeum: point deduction
gamsa hamnida: thank you
googup hwal bop: accupressure
goorugi: rolling/tumbling
guk-gi: flag
gup: rank (for color belts)
him: inner strength/life force energy
hosinsool: self-defense
jeon: round (competition segment)
jeum: point
jongsin-tongil: meditation
ki-hop: yell/the power sound that combines physical and mental energy
kwan: school where Tae Kwon Do is taught
kyong-go: penalty
kyorugi: sparring
kyuk pah: breaking
poomse: forms (formal exercises)
seung: winner
shi-gan: time (time out)
shim ho hyup: breathing control

GLOSSARY

ENGLISH–KOREAN

about face: dorra
arc-hand: agwi-son
arc-hand strike: agwi-son chi-gi
arm: pol
attention: cha-ryot
attention stance: cha-ryot sogi
axe kick: chik-gi
back: dwi
back-fist: dung-joomock
back-fist strike: dung-joomock chi-gi
back-hand: son-dung
back kick: dwi cha-gi
back stance: dwi-gubi sogi
ball of foot: ahpchook
basic: ki bon
basic form: ki bon poomse
bear-hand: kom-son
begin: si-jak
block: maggi
body: momtong
bow: kyong-ye
breathing control: shim ho hyup
break (stop): kalyeo
breaking: kyuk pah
chest protector: ka soom ho goo
containing vital energy stance: po jumok sogi
continue: kae sok
crane stance: haktari sogi

crescent kick: bandul cha-gi
deduction of point: gam jum
diamond block: kumkang maggi
double: narae
double block: narae maggi
double kick: narae cha-gi
double knife-hand block: son-nal maggi
double punch: du jumok chirugi
down block/low block: ahre maggi
eight: yodul
eighth: pul
elbow: palkoop
elbow strike: palkoop chi-gi
energy (internal energy or life-force): him
face: eolgul
face block/rising block: eolgul maggi (also wee maggi)
fifth: oh
fingertip: son-kut
first: el
fist: joomock
five: dasot
flag: guk-gi
fly/flying: ye tan
flying kick: ye tan cha-gi
foot: baal
forearm: palmock
form (formal exercise): poomse
four: net

fourth: sa
front: ahp
front stance: ahp-gubi sogi
front rising kick: ahp-bodo alligi (or ahp-cha olligi)
front snap kick: ahp cha-gi
front thrust kick: ahp-jillo cha-gi
good-bye: ahn-nyonghi gasip-siyo (to the one who leaves), ahn-nyonghi gesipsiyo (to the one who stays)
grand master: kwanjangnim (seventh to ninth degree)
groin defense: noollo maggi
gymnasium (a place for the study of Tae Kwon Do): dojang
hammer-fist: me-joomok
hammer fist strike: me-joomok chi-gi
hand: son
head: mo-li
healing (accupressure): googup hwal bop
heel: dwi-chook
hello: ahn-nyong
high: wee
high block: wee maggi
hold/stop: gu-mahn
holding: jupgi
hook: tol
hook kick: huryo cha-gi
hook punch: huryo chi-gi

horseback riding stance: ju-
   choom sogi
how are you?: ahn-nyong
   hasimnika
in/inner: ahn
inner arm block: ahn maggi
instep: baaldung
instructor (first to third degree
   black belt): chokyonim
judge: bu sim
jump/jumping: yo
jumping double front kick:
   dubal pulryo cha-gi
jumping kick: yo cha-gi
juror: bae sim
jumping kick: yo cha-gi
kick: cha-gi
knee: moo-rup
knee strike: moo-rup chi-gi
kneeling: kool o-angi
knife-foot: baal-nul
knife-hand: son-nal
knife-hand strike: son-nal
   chi-gi
knuckle-fist: pyon-joomock
knuckle-fist strike: pyon-
   joomock chi-gi
left: wen
leg: dari
life-force: him
lotus position (yoga seated
   posture): baro-angi
low: ahre
low block/down block: ahre
   maggi
master (fourth to sixth degree
   black belt): sabomnim
martial art/moral culture/way
   of life: do
meditation: jongsin-tongil
middle: gaunde
middle block: momtong
   maggi
mountain block: santil
   maggi
mouth: ip

neck: mok
nine: ahob
ninth: koo
one: hana
out/outer: backat
outer arm block: ahn palmok
   pakhag maggi
palm-heel: batang-son
palm-heel block: batang-son
   maggi
palm-heel strike: batang-son
   chi-gi
partial mountain block: ur-
   santil maggi
penalty: kyong-go
point: jeum
point deduction: gam-jeum
protruding knuckle: bam
   joomok
protruding knuckle strike:
   bam joomok chi-gi
punch: chirugi
push/pushing: mil-ya
pushing kick: mil-ya cha-gi
rank: gup (color belt levels),
   dan (black belt levels)
ready: joonbi
ready stance: pyong-sogi
recorder: ki rohk
referee: joo sim
return: barro
reverse outer arm block:
   pakhag maggi
reverse punch: paro chirugi
ridge-hand: son-nal dung
ridge-hand strike: son-nal
   dung chi-gi
right: o-ruen
rising block/face block: eolgul
   maggi
rolling/tumbling: goorugi
round (motion): dolryo
round (competition segment):
   jeon
roundhouse kick: dolryo
   cha-gi

school (a place where Tae
   Kwon Do is taught):
   kwan
scissors block: kawi maggi
second: e
self-defense: hosinsool
seven: ilgub
seventh: chil
side: yop
side punch: yop chirugi
side rising kick: yop-bodo
   olligi
side snap kick: yop cha-gi
side thrust kick: yop-jillo
   cha-gi
single knife-hand block: han
   son-nal maggi
six: yasot
sixth: yuk
spar/sparring: kyorugi
spear-fingers: pyon son-kut
spear-fingers strike: pyon
   son-kut chi-gi
spin/spinning: momtong
   dolryo
spinning kick: momtong
   dolryo cha-gi
spinning strike: tol gae chi-gi
spreading block: hecho
   maggi
square punch: tol chi-gi
stance: sogi
stop: gu-mahn
strike: chi-gi
switch: ba-quo
ten: yol
tenth: sib
thank you: gamsa hamnida
three: set
throw/throwing: donsigi
thrust/thrusting: jirugi
third: sam
tiger stance: bumsogi
time: shi gan
timer: kae sim
tumbling/rolling: goorugi

turn around/about face: dorra
twisted stance: koa-sogi
two: dul
uniform (for Tae Kwon Do training): dobok
walking stance: ahp sogi
waist: huri
way of life/moral culture/martial art: do
win: seung
wrist: sonmock
X block: yeot pero maggi
yell (to collect and focus internal energy): ki-hop
you are welcome: chonmaney

KOREAN–ENGLISH

agwi-son: arc-hand
agwi-son chi-gi: arc-hand strike
ahn: in/inner
ahn-nyung: hello
ahn maggi: inner block
ahn-nyonghi gasipsiyo: good-bye (to the one who leaves)
ahn-nyonghi gesipsiyo: good-bye (to the one who stays)
ahn-nyong hasimnika: how are you?
ahn maggi: inner arm block
ahn palmok pakhag maggi: outer arm block
ahob: nine
ahp: front
ahp-bodo olligi: front rising kick
ahp-cha olligi: front rising kick
ahp cha-gi: front snap kick
ahnchook: ball of foot
ahp-gubi sogi: front stance
ahp-jillo cha-gi: front thrust kick

ahp-jumok chirugi: jab punch
ahp sogi: walking stance
ahre: low
ahre maggi: low block/down block
baal: foot
baaldung: instep
baalnul: knife-foot
bae sim: juror
backat: out/outer
backat maggi: outer block
bam joomok: protruding knuckle
bam joomok chi-gi: protruding knuckle strike
bandul cha-gi: crescent kick
ba-quo: switch
baro-angi: lotus position (seated yoga position)
barro: return
batang-son: palm-heel
batang-son chi-gi: palm-heel strike
batang-son maggi: palm-heel block
bumsogi: tiger stance
bu sim: judge
cha-gi: kick
cha-ryot: attention
cha-ryot sogi: attention stance
chi-gi: punch/strike
chik-gi: axe kick
chil: seventh
chokyonim: instructor (first to third degree black belt)
chonmaneyo: you are welcome
dan: rank/degree (black belts)
dari: leg
dasot: five
do: way of life/martial art/moral culture
dobok: uniform (for Tae

Kwon Do practice)
dolryo: round (motion)
dolryo cha-gi: roundhouse kick
dojang: gymnasium (for Tae Kwon Do practice)
donzigi: throw/throwing
dorra: about face/turn around
dubal pulryo cha-gi: jumping double front kick
du jumok chirugi: double punch
dul: two
dung-joomock: back-fist
dung-joomock chi-gi: back-fist strike
dwi: back
dwi cha-gi: back kick
dwi-chook: heel
dwi-gubi sogi: back stance
e: second
el: first
eolgul: face
eolgul maggi: face block/rising block
gam jeum: point deduction
gamsa hamnida: thank you
gaunde: middle
googup hwal bop: accupressure
goorugi: rolling/tumbling
guk-gi: flag
gu-mahn: stop/hold
gup: rank (color belts only)
haktari-sogi: crane stance
hanna: one
han sonnal maggi: knife-hand block
hecho maggi: spreading block
him: life force enersgy
hosinsool: self-defense
huri: waist
huryo cha-gi: hook kick
ilgub: seven

ip: mouth

jeon: round (competition segment)

jeum: point

jirugi: thrust/thrusting

jongsin-tongil: meditation

joomock: fist

joonbi: (get) ready

joo sim: referee

juchoom-sogi: horseback riding stance

jupgi: holding

kae sim: timer

kae sok: continue

kalyeo: break/stop

ka soom ho goo: chest protector

kawi maggi: scissors block

ki bon: basic

ki bon poomse: basic form

ki-hop: yell (to collect and focus internal energy)

ki rohk: recorder

koa-sogi: twisted stance/hook stance

kom-son: bear-hand

kom-son chi-gi: bear-hand strike

koo: ninth

kumkang maggi: diamond block

kwan: school (where Tae Kwon Do is taught)

kwanjangnim: grand master (fourth to sixth degree black belt)

kyong-go: penalty

kyong-ye: bow

kyorugi: spar/sparring

kyuk pah: breaking

maggi: block

me-joomock: hammer-fist

me-joomock chi-gi: hammer fist strike

mil-ya cha-gi: pushing kick

mock: arm

mo-li: head

momtong: body

momtong dolryo: spin/spinning

momtong dolryo cha-gi: spinning kick

moo-rup: knee

moo-rup chi-gi: knee strike

narae: double

narae cha-gi: double kick

narae chi-gi: double strike

narae maggi: double block

net: four

noollo maggi: groin defense

oh: fifth

o-ruen: right

pakhag maggi: reverse outer arm block

palkoop: elbow

palkoop chi-gi: elbow strike

palmock: forearm

paro chirugi: reverse punch

po jumok sogi: containing vital energy stance

poomse: form/formal exercise

pul: eighth

pyongi-sogi: ready stance

pyon-joomock: knuckle fist

pyon-joomock chi-gi: knuckle fist strike

pyon son-kut: spear-fingers

pyon son-kut chi-gi: spear-fingers strike

sa: fourth

sabomnim: master (fourth to sixth degree black belt)

sam: third

santil maggi: mountain block

set: three

shi gan: time

shim ho hyup: breathing control

sib: tenth

si-jak: begin

sogi: stance

son: hand

son-dung: back-hand

son-kut: fingertip

sonmock: wrist

son-nal: knife-hand

son-nal chi-gi: knife-hand strike

son-nal dung: ridge-hand/-reverse knife-hand

son-nal dung chi-gi: ridge-hand strike

son-nal maggi: double knife-hand block

tol gae: hook

tol chi-gi: hook punch

ur-santil maggi: partial mountain block

wee: high

wee maggi: high block

yasot: six

yeot pero maggi: X block

ye tan: flying

ye tan cha-gi: flying kick

yo: jump/jumping

yo cha-gi: jumping kick

yodul: eight

yol: ten

yop: side

yop-bodo olligi: side rising kick

yop cha-gi: side snap kick

yop chirugi: side punch

yop-jillo cha-gi: side thrust kick

yuk: sixth

INDEX

(

```
796.815 Par
Park, Yeon Hwan.
Black belt taekwondo :

$35.00  09/13/00  AGK-4854
```

DATE DUE